Christy Lane's
Complete Book of
Line Dancing

Christy Lane
Spokane, WA

Human Kinetics

Library of Congress Cataloging-in-Publication Data

Lane, Christy.
    [Complete book of line dancing]
    Christy Lane's complete book of line dancing / Christy Lane.
        p.   cm.
    ISBN 0-87322-719-0
    1. Line dancing.   I. Title.   II. Title. Complete book of line dancing.
GV1768.L35   1995
793.3--dc20   94-18038
                                                                              CIP

ISBN: 0-87322-719-0

Developmental Editor: Julia Anderson; **Assistant Editors:** Jacqueline Blakley and Julie Marx; **Copyeditor:** Ginger Rodriguez; **Proofreader:** Matt Scholz; **Text Design, Typesetting, and Layout:** Doug Burnett; **Cover Designer:** Jack Davis; **Photographer (cover and interior):** Pete Moroz; **Illustrator:** Doug Burnett; **Printer:** United Graphics

Human Kinetics books are available at special discounts for bulk purchase. Special editions or book excerpts can also be created to specification. For details, contact the Special Sales Manager at Human Kinetics.

Printed in the United States of America   10   9   8   7   6   5   4

Human Kinetics
Web site: http://www.humankinetics.com/

United States: Human Kinetics, P.O. Box 5076, Champaign, IL 61825-5076
1-800-747-4457
e-mail: humank@hkusa.com

Canada: Human Kinetics, Box 24040, Windsor, ON N8Y 4Y9
1-800-465-7301 (in Canada only)
e-mail: humank@hkcanada.com

Europe: Human Kinetics, P.O. Box IW14, Leeds LS16 6TR, United Kingdom
(44) 1132 781708
e-mail: humank@hkeurope.com

Australia: Human Kinetics, 57A Price Avenue, Lower Mitcham, South Australia 5062
(08) 277 1555
e-mail: humank@hkaustralia.com

New Zealand: Human Kinetics, P.O. Box 105-231, Auckland 1
(09) 523 3462
e-mail: humank@hknewz.com

Contents

Welcome to Line Dancing!

As I fastened my seat belt on another 747, I could feel a warmth in my heart as I reminisced over the previous days' events. I had just wrapped up teaching line dance at a state convention. One of my jobs was to host and teach at the Friday night social. Hundreds of people showed up, of all ages and abilities, ready to learn this big dance craze—line dancing. And what a night it was! To take an empty room and fill it with energy, excitement, music, laughter, fun, and challenge was an incredible experience. The most amazing part of it was watching everyone dance. Ability level, age, and gender made no difference. It was wonderful. The next morning I received many inspired greetings—first-timers' faces came alive as they shared their new adventures into the world of dance. The more experienced dancers were moving quite slowly through the hallways after dancing their legs off till dawn.

As I looked out the airplane window at a beautiful sunset above the clouds, I thought how lucky I was to be given the good fortune to share this wonderful dance form with so many people. Over and over again I have seen dance become a tremendous outlet—physical, mental, emotional, social, and spiritual—a marvelous way to experience life. And now I have the opportunity to share dance with you in this book—to inform you, motivate you, and provide you with a great personal reference guide for line dancing.

Chapter 1 is especially for beginners—it includes fun, practical suggestions to eliminate the fear of the dance floor and get you up and moving. Floor etiquette is defined as well as proper dance alignment. This chapter also presents the history of line dance and its place as a dance form among the other dance disciplines. Chapter 2 will get you ready to dance by introducing you to terminology and how to read a "foot map."

You will start moving in chapter 3, learning the beginning line dances. The dances I've selected for this book were the most popular national dances at the time of this writing. When you master these, you are on your way to chapter 4, where you will learn intermediate-level dances, and chapter 5, which presents more advanced dances.

If you are looking for variety or challenge, the rest of the book will keep you stimulated. Chapter 6 introduces couples pattern dancing, which is line dancing with a partner! The mixers and icebreakers are excellent for making parties and socials come alive. Chapter 7 focuses on tips for dancers, highlighting style, confidence, and enjoyment. I explain various exercises, such as hip isolations, to help you do your hip rolls on dances like the Tush Push!

The last chapter is especially designed for teachers. If you are a line dance instructor or interested in becoming one, you will appreciate the information in chapter 8. Equipment, music sources, and class format are just some of the topics I cover. The appendixes give a complete list of popular line dances and a list of music so you can practice dancing your heart out!

Now put on your dancin' shoes, partner, cuz you're in for a good time!

Acknowledgments

A very special thank-you to Brian Tibbetts, Pete Moroz, Mike Kennedy, Trish Berg, Scott Bassett, Lorna Hamilton, and Brad Pressman for their support, enthusiasm, and personal attention on this project.

I would also like to thank the models who appear in the photos: Karine Freeze, Maité Gorrindo, Ronda Hendren, Tina Marie Hill, Scott Hough, Mercedes Klein, Elaine Magee, Bill Magee, Chad Mitchell, Melissa Montague, Victor Paternoster, Wendy Rincon, Mike Roth, Jeannie Standal, Brian Tibbetts, Wendy Tobert, and Jennifer Vinta.

And to all the line dancers I have met throughout the country—thanks for the good times!

Dedicated to Victor, Mark, Eleanor Joan, Mary, Steve, Eleanor, Nick, and Dolores, for their unconditional support.

Would You Like to Dance?

What a great time to be alive! We are in the middle of one of the biggest dance crazes ever—as big as the jitterbug was in the 1950s and the twist in the '60s. Just think, you could have been born in another era and never had the opportunity to learn line dancing! So congratulations for being alive *now* . . . because you are about to make history.

First let me introduce myself. I am your personal line dance instructor, the one crazy enough to create all the little feet you are about to see. And you? You must be either a beginning dancer embarking on an exciting adventure into the world of dance or an experienced line dancer in search of current information. If you are experienced, feel free to go right to chapter 2. If you are my Rookie of the Year, not even sure if this is where your dreams will come true, hang on and read on, because I have some news for you! If you're looking for suggestions to keep you inspired as you work your way through the dances, stick with me because I have some pointers coming up in the next few pages. But first, I want to tell you a little about the history of line dancing and explain why it's so popular today.

What's All This Ruckus About Line Dancing?

Line dancing is like all other dance forms, a reflection of history and culture. Dance itself has been a form of communication and self-expression since prehistoric times. People have enjoyed dance not only as an art form but as a way to feel good physically, to be mentally stimulated, to develop self-esteem, and to meet people. For some, dance is even part of the path to spiritual enlightenment.

If you asked 10 different people with some knowledge of dance when line dancing began, you'd probably get 10 different answers. A popular opinion about line dancing is that it is not a fad but a tradition. Some believe this style of dancing has strong ties to folk dancing. In the 1800s European immigrants traveled west to North America, bringing with them a wealth of culture in their native dances, such as the polka and waltz, whose movements joined and evolved into what was called round and square dancing. Cowboys on the western frontier from the 1860s to the 1890s took these more traditional dance moves and assimilated them into the country-western style; they are credited with the simple footwork and the country flair reflecting the culture of their time. In the early 1900s, folk dancing was brought into the schools through physical education programs. As large numbers of youth learned country-western dance, its popularity grew in leisure and social activities.

Others believe line dancing evolved from the disco era. The movie *Saturday Night Fever*, released in 1978, caused a dance sensation. As the lines between pop and country were blurring, actor and dancer John Travolta did it again in 1980 with the movie *Urban Cowboy*, which spurred a new wave of western fashion, music, and dance. With the media behind it, country influence began to sweep through grass-roots America in the early 1990s. Line dancing rose to the forefront when the country-western "Achy Breaky Heart" became the most popular song in 1993. Savvy marketers packaged Billy Ray

Cyrus and his tune with a new line dance, which swept the country. Some say that "Achy Breaky Heart" was a turning point in the popularity of line dance.

Today line dance is crossing boundaries of income, race, age, and sexual orientation. Singles as well as families see line dancing as a healthy social outlet. Numerous opportunities exist for recreational dancing at dance clubs, convention socials, wedding receptions, school-sponsored dances, studio recitals, and dance competitions. Line dance now incorporates many musical styles—jazz, rock, and disco have all made contributions to country dance and music. Line dances are performed not only to country music, but to rock and rap as well.

The country-western craze of the 1990s is demonstrating staying power. Country music has crossed over to the pop charts. New line dances and variations are popping up everywhere. Regional variations of the same line dances make the original version questionable, but they are all popular.

Why this big attraction to line dance today? Part of the appeal stems from a growing interest in the country way of life. We are attracted to the simplicity of the American frontier past and both the rugged individualism and close family ties that it represents. Because line dancing is easier than other fad dances, the whole family can participate, helping this art form combine opportunities for individualization with the camaraderie of the community dance hall.

Now line dancing is considered a dance art form of its own, with its own terminology and standardized steps. Its patterned foot movements are usually done to a set number of counts per sequence and then the sequence is repeated, sometimes facing another direction. A social and economic culture has evolved out of country-western dance events, competitions, trade magazines, and television shows. The popularity of this widely accepted dance form also has grown enormously internationally. The origin of line dance may not be clear, but one thing is: Line dance is here today.

Five Steps to Success

The best thing about line dancing is that *you can't lose!* Because line dancing does not require a partner, you do not have to cringe in anticipation of that scary question, "Do you wanna dance?" That's right, no more! When you hear the music, hit the floor. (No, not literally, I mean get on the dance floor and start moving!) It doesn't matter what your age or ability level is, everybody dances with everybody—line dancing is performed with a group of people moving in unison (most of the time in straight lines facing the same direction) to music while having a blast! To get the most out of line dancing, take the following five steps.

Think Positively

Now, because of your desire to get out there on the dance floor and look good soon, there's not enough time to tell you throughout the book how great, wonderful, beautiful, individual, and expressive you are. So it's up to you. Do it now. What are you thinking of this very moment? Are you doubting yourself? If you're planning on going through all that negative stuff, hurry up, I'm waiting. We have things to do, mountains to climb, bridges to cross, and line dancing to learn! You can wait until you're 100 years old to dance, but honestly, I don't have that kind of time and besides, if you start now, just think how good you'll be at 100! OK, take a deep breath and then breathe out that negativity . . . right now. This is the age of the body-mind connection. So, let's get into the right attitude. You will be 100% more effective if you think positively. This is the time to tell your body, "Fred Astaire, here I come!"

Start at the Beginning

I know, some people are born dancers. But you cannot be intimidated by them. When you look onto the dance floor, where do your eyes usually go? To the more advanced (skilled) dancers, the ones you think are naturals. *Wrong.* Most of them started the same way you did—from the beginning—and they practiced, practiced, and practiced some more. That's the key. Of course there are the "born dancers" out there, but not very many. If you really look around the next time you go out, you will find people falling, tripping, and stepping on toes. Nine times out of 10, they will be laughing! You have to have a good sense of humor whenever you try anything the first time. So come on, smile . . . relax . . . you have to start somewhere. Fortunately, you picked a dance form that is easy to learn. (Thank heavens we do not have to spin on our heads!) Good—you are halfway there.

Go in the Right Direction

If you have ever driven the Los Angeles freeways, line dancing is a piece of cake! You're bound to bump into someone. If that should happen, smile, be courteous, and continue on. (Besides, stepping on a foot is an interesting way to meet someone new!) Just as the freeway belongs to everyone, so does the dance floor. Of course it always helps to know which direction to go, and that's where floor etiquette comes into the picture (see Figure 1.1). Line dancing is usually done in the middle of the dance floor in an imaginary rectangular space with everyone facing the same direction unless the dance club or hostess designates another location. This tiny bit of knowledge will really keep you from colliding with people! Take note that all the partner dancers move counterclockwise around the dance floor in what is called the "line of dance." Ahhh, so that's it! Now that you know how to "drive" the dancing "freeway," shorten up those steps! This will make you more agile and mobile. Line dancing participants will be starting on the same foot and moving in the same direction (thank goodness). So there's nothing to worry about. When everyone goes right, you go right!

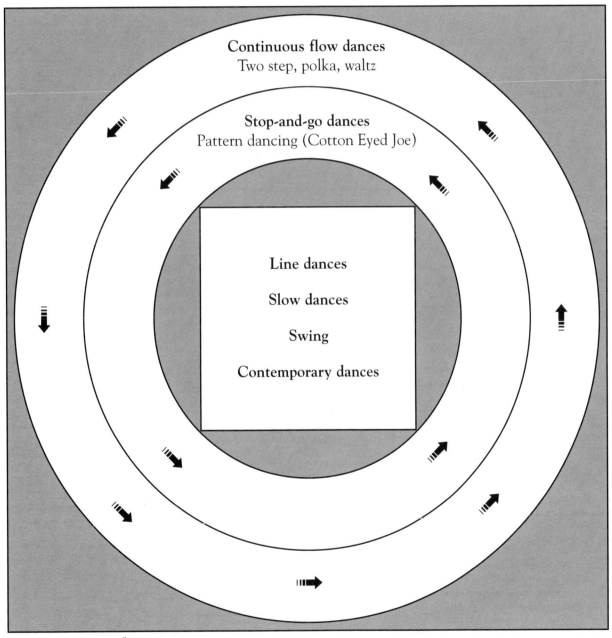

Continuous flow dances
Two step, polka, waltz

Stop-and-go dances
Pattern dancing (Cotton Eyed Joe)

Line dances

Slow dances

Swing

Contemporary dances

Figure 1.1 *Dance floor etiquette.*

Stand Tall

No, this is not your mother speaking. Proper alignment allows you to use your muscles most efficiently and with the least amount of tension. Besides all that, you look better. Do me a favor: Stand against a wall. Put your heels against the wall and pull your shoulders back so that your body is in alignment. Try pressing the small of the back into the wall as you lift your stomach and rib cage up and in. Are you breathing? You can think clearer and move faster if you breathe. (Besides that, you won't pass out.) Stop . . . close your eyes and feel this position. Practice this little exercise for good body awareness. Lift your chin so it is parallel to the floor. Are you biting your tongue? Wiggle your fingers so I know you are relaxed. Now, walk forward away from the wall and see if you can maintain your posture. Don't look down! Looking at your feet while dancing will only make you dizzy, and you will miss the wonderful scenery. Besides, the ants have their own thing going on down there! Now practice walking backward, at your own pace. Try walking forward and back taking smaller steps.

Did you ever get in trouble when you were a kid for standing around and putting your hands in your pockets? Well, no more—this is your chance! The standard arm position for guys in line dancing is thumbs in the pockets, and for the ladies it is a relaxed fist at waist or hip level. It is also acceptable to have relaxed arms by your sides. Go ahead now and try walking with your arms in either one of the positions. You're on a roll!

Have Fun

Line dancing is a great stress reducer, not a stress enhancer! The benefits are enormous. First off you cannot possibly think of anything else when your mind is on memorizing steps. What a great way to take your mind off _____ (you fill in the blank). Line dancing can be an emotional release, especially when you let yourself go in the music. It is also good exercise, just like low-impact aerobics. Speaking of aerobics, the health clubs around the country today are teaching line dancing like crazy. Line dancing is a great way to blend exercise and recreation, because you can raise your heart rate up to 60% to 70% of its maximum, which builds stamina safely. All you have to do to achieve an aerobic benefit is to gradually increase the amount of time you dance continuously. Start with one song and gradually add more tunes until you are dancing 15 to 60 minutes nonstop three times per week. The best part about line dancing is that it is a super way to meet new people and experience great personal satisfaction from your accomplishment.

OK, so do we have our mental act together? Are you standing tall? Are you breathing? Are you thinking positively? Well then, let's do it!

Know Your Lingo

Before you hit the dance floor to practice the steps you'll find in the following chapters, there are a few things you should know. Most important are knowing how to read the foot maps that follow and understanding the lingo they're written in! This chapter will help you out in these all-important areas.

How to Read a Foot Map

Reading a foot map is very similar to reading a road map, as long as you know what direction you are going in and what all those little symbols mean! All the dance illustrations in this book read left to right. When you see an arrow, follow the direction it is pointing. It's that easy. The following key defines all the symbols on the foot maps. For example, the foot pictured with a solid line is just like the solid line on a freeway map. It's the best way to go, so put your weight on it! And the rest stops are even illustrated for you! Of course, the rest stops in this book are slightly different from the ones on a road map. They are easily marked by the word *hold* and that's exactly what you do . . . nothing. (These rests are great opportunities to "get your head together" for your next step.)

Have a look here at an example of your dancing road map and the key to symbols.

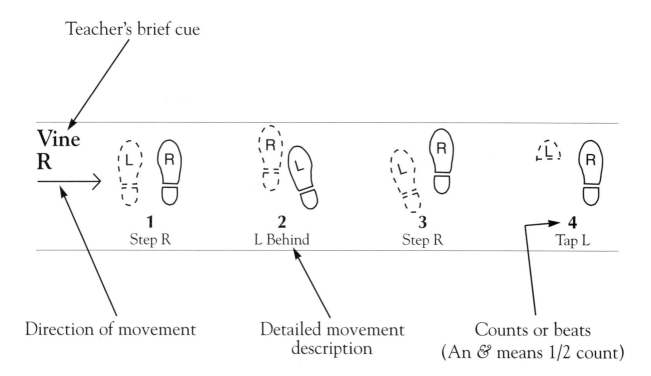

Key to symbols

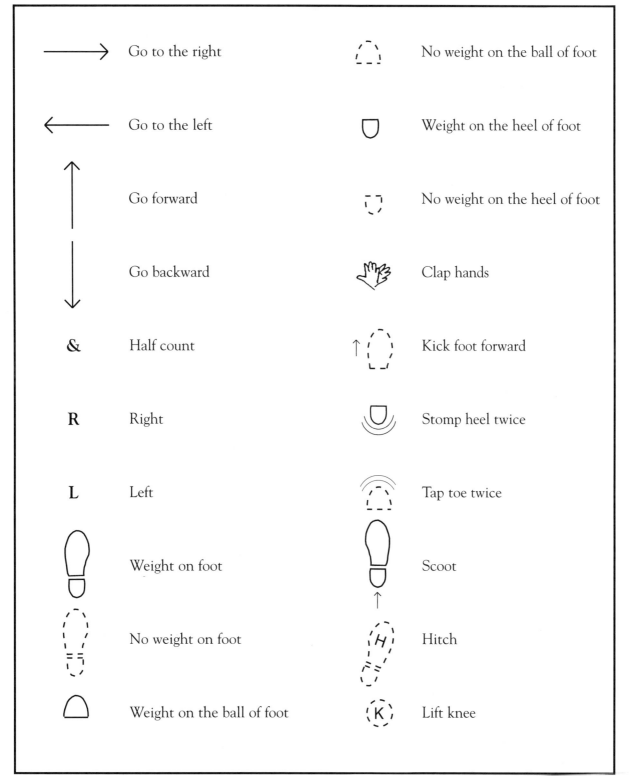

⟶ Go to the right	No weight on the ball of foot
⟵ Go to the left	Weight on the heel of foot
Go forward	No weight on the heel of foot
Go backward	Clap hands
& Half count	Kick foot forward
R Right	Stomp heel twice
L Left	Tap toe twice
Weight on foot	Scoot
No weight on foot	Hitch
Weight on the ball of foot	Lift knee

Line Dancing Terminology

Want to make an impression the next time you go dancing? Try using lingo such as "grapevines," "scoots," "swivels," and "hooks," then suggest how well everyone does the "hitch kick" and see what happens! Here's the lingo to assist you in learning your dances. Maybe you can write it on the palm of your hand in case you need a quick reference next time you are out on the town! Good luck!

accent—Special emphasis to a movement or a heavy beat in music.

and—Half of a count or a quick count. For example, "one and two" or "and one two." Noted in foot maps with an ampersand (&).

ball change—A change of weight from the ball of one foot to the ball of the other foot.

begin—The start of the dance.

brush—A brushing or sweeping movement of the foot against the floor.

brush-fan—Brushing the foot forward and to the side in one continuous movement.

center—The dancer's balancing point in proper alignment, also known as *starting point*.

cha-cha—Five steps to four beats of music beginning with either the left or right foot. The rhythm is slow, slow, quick, quick, slow. (Also known as a three-step pattern—see *shuffle*.) For example,

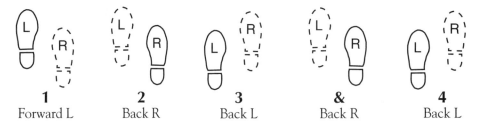

1	**2**	**3**	**&**	**4**
Forward L	Back R	Back L	Back R	Back L

charleston—A four-step pattern with four beats. For example,

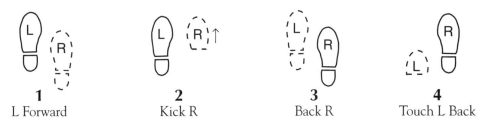

1	**2**	**3**	**4**
L Forward	Kick R	Back R	Touch L Back

chaîné turn—A traveling 360-degree turn on the balls of the feet taking four steps to complete. When starting on the right foot, turn to the right. Can be done in multiple.

chassé—A three-step pattern to two beats: step, together, step to the side, front, or back. The free foot never passes the supporting foot.

choreography—Arranging or planning dance movements into routines.

chug—See *scoot*.

clockwise—See *reverse line of dance (RLOD)*.

close—To bring feet together.

counterclockwise—See *line of dance (LOD)*.

cross—One foot moves in front or back of the other.

CW—An abbreviation for country-western.

diagonal—A movement left or right at 45 degrees from center, facing one wall.

dig—Touching the ball or heel of the nonsupporting foot with a strong emphasis.

dip—A slight bend of the support knee keeping the other knee straight.

drag—See *draw.*

draw—To bring the nonsupporting free foot slowly together to the supporting foot.

grapevine—A four-step traveling move to four beats that goes right or left. Also referred to as *vine.* The fourth step in a grapevine can be a touch, brush, kick, or similar step. Grapevines can also be continuous, alternating crossing in front or in back. (Eight grapevine steps or more in one direction is often called a *weave.*) For example,

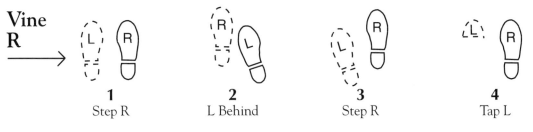

half turn—A 180-degree turn to the left or right performed in two beats of music. For example,

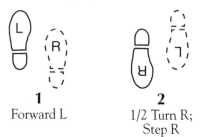

heel—Tap the floor with the heel of the foot.

heel fan—With feet together, rotate one heel out and return to center, keeping toes together. For example,

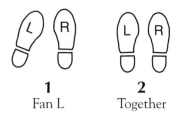

heel pivot—A turn on the heel of one foot with no weight change.

heel splits—With feet together and weight on the balls of both feet, push both heels apart on count 1 and bring heels together on count 2. Also known as *pigeon toe.*

heel stomps—Stomp the heels to the floor with a rapid motion.

hip bump—An emphasized hip movement in any given direction.

hitch—Lift the knee and cross the supporting foot in front with heel showing. Also known as *hook.*

hitch kick—A kick ball change.

hitch turn—Hitch and turn together using hitch momentum to carry through turn.

hold—Counting off a designated time or number of beats before taking another step.

hook—See *hitch*.

hook turn—A 360-degree turn performed on the ball of one foot. Also known as a *pirouette* or *spin*.

hop—Start with weight on supporting foot, jump, and land on same foot.

hop change—Begin with one heel forward; in one beat, hop and switch to the other heel forward.

jazz box—Also called a *jazz square*. This is a four-count move and can be performed to the left or right. For example,

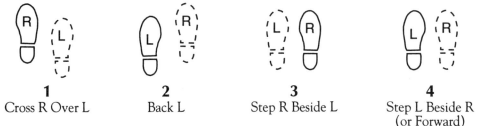

1	**2**	**3**	**4**
Cross R Over L	Back L	Step R Beside L	Step L Beside R (or Forward)

kick—A quick foot movement (kick) forward, backward, or sideways without a transfer of weight.

knee dip—From closed position, bend both knees, then straighten.

line of dance (LOD)—The counterclockwise circular movement of dancers around the dance floor. Dancing in a clockwise direction is called *reverse line of dance (RLOD)*.

lock—A tight cross of the feet.

military full turn—After a military half turn, step forward and pivot another 180 degrees in the opposite direction in two beats of music.

military half turn—Step out on either the right or left foot and make a 180-degree turn in the opposite direction in one beat of music.

outside chainé turn—A chainé turn to the opposite direction. For example, if traveling right, turn to the left. Also known as a *spiral turn*.

over—To step across the weighted foot.

paddle turn—A quarter, half, three-quarter, or full turn shifting the weight from one foot to another.

pas de bourrée—See *sailor steps*.

pigeon toe—See *heel splits*.

pirouette—See *hook turn*.

pivot—See *half turn*. (Sometimes referred to as a *partial chainé turn*.)

plié—A bend of the knees.

point—Stretching the toes of the free foot so the foot "points" forward, backward, sideways, or crosswise.

polka step—Similar to a shuffle, but done in a more bouncy and lively style with the feet farther off the floor.

quarter turn—A 90-degree turn to the left or right.

reverse line of dance (RLOD)—The clockwise circular movement of dancers around the dance floor.

rock—Shifting the weight from foot to foot.

sailor steps—A three-step shuffle pattern to two beats of music. Also known as a *pas de bourrée*. For example,

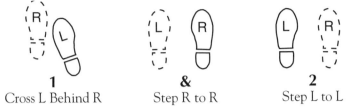

1	**&**	**2**
Cross L Behind R	Step R to R	Step L to L

scissors—See *toe splits*.

scoot—Traveling in the air while hopping on the supporting leg forward, backward, or sideways with the other leg in a hook position. Also known as a *chug*.

scuff—Strike the floor with the heel with greater force than a brush.

shuffle—Also known as a *triple step* or *cha-cha*. Can be performed forward, backward, or sideways. Counted as "one and two." The second step can pass, be beside, or be behind (most common) the first step. For example,

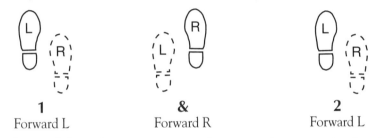

1	**&**	**2**
Forward L	Forward R	Forward L

slide—Step on one foot and draw the nonsupporting foot up to the supporting foot in a dragging movement.

spin—See *hook turn*.

spiral turn—See *outside chainé turn*.

spot—A technique used to avoid dizziness resulting from a series of fast turns. Focus your eyes on one spot for as long as possible when turning.

step—Transfer weight from one foot to the other.

stomp—Hit the floor with the whole foot or heel. You may step on the foot or rebound and use the same foot for the next movement.

strut—A two-count walk performed by stepping on the heel, then the toe.

swing—Raise the free foot and move forward, backward, to the side, or crosswise.

switch—A quick shift of weight from one foot to the other. Normally done with a heel.

swivel—With feet together, turn on the balls of the foot right or left and rotate hips side to side. For example,

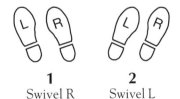

1	**2**
Swivel R	Swivel L

tap or **touch**—The toe of free foot taps or touches the floor without a weight change. For example,

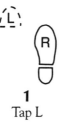

1
Tap L

tempo—Speed of the beat of music.

toe fan—With feet together, the toe of one foot moves outward to one side and back to center. For example,

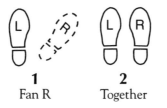

1   **2**
Fan R   Together

toe splits—With feet together and weight on heels of both feet, push toes apart on count 1. Bring toes together on count 2. Also known as *scissors*.

together—Bring feet together with weight evenly distributed on both feet.

triple step—See *shuffle*.

turn—A rotation of the body, taking one or more steps to complete.

variations—Movements of footwork that vary from the indicated dance patterns.

vine—See *grapevine*.

weave—A continuous grapevine of six or more counts, sometimes referred to as a traveling grapevine.

Heel, Toe, Heel, Toe—Here We Go!

Beginning Line Dances

OK, here we go. Let's start with some beginning line dances. What makes a line dance suitable for beginners? The first consideration is the length of the dance (the total number of steps). The dances in this chapter are 16 to 32 counts, and most end in multiples of 8 counts. It is easy to repeat the sequence at the end of an 8 count because we naturally count beats of music in eights. Next, most of the steps are performed in one beat of music; more intricate steps in the advanced dances require two steps to one beat. Also, beginning dances have limited changes of direction during the basic movement pattern.

When you are learning a dance, try focusing on one other dancer if you need help remembering the next move (hopefully your person will not lead you astray!). Line dances are done one wall, two wall, or four wall. After you perform the sequence pattern once, you will end facing a different direction (or wall) before repeating the sequence. Sound confusing? Don't be alarmed—just relax and repeat the exact same sequence facing the new direction. (Remember, if everyone goes right, you go right!) If you only face two walls during the repeated sequences, you are performing a two-wall dance. If your sequence faces four walls, then you are performing a four-wall dance. There are, of course, one-wall dances that continuously repeat the sequence facing front. (Isn't that nice?)

Learn one dance at a time, go at your own pace, and practice, practice, practice. Remember that a few steps performed well are better than several steps done sloppily. And a pointer about music—be sure to select a slow pace when you are first learning a dance. Then change to a faster pace once you have mastered it. A list of suggested practice music is provided in Appendix B; always use music you enjoy! It is beyond the scope of this book to discuss music and rhythms in detail. Consider taking a music class if you want to know more, or when you go to a dance, listen to the music being played and make a note of it. Your homework for this week is practical application. Go out and try the dances!

Cowboy Motion

Begin

Vine R →

1	2	3	4
Step R	L Behind	Step R	Tap L

Vine L ←

5	6	7	8
Step L	R Behind	Step L	Tap R

Go Back

9	10	11	12
Step Back R	Step Back L	Step Back R	Stomp L

Toe Taps

13, 14	15, 16	17	18	19	20
Tap L Toe Side Twice	Tap L Heel Twice	Tap L Toe Once	Tap L Heel Once	Switch Feet	Hold

Hips

21	22	23	24
Rock Forward	Rock Back	Rock Forward	Rock Back

Quarter turn to the left as you repeat the entire dance. This is a four-wall dance.

Bus Stop

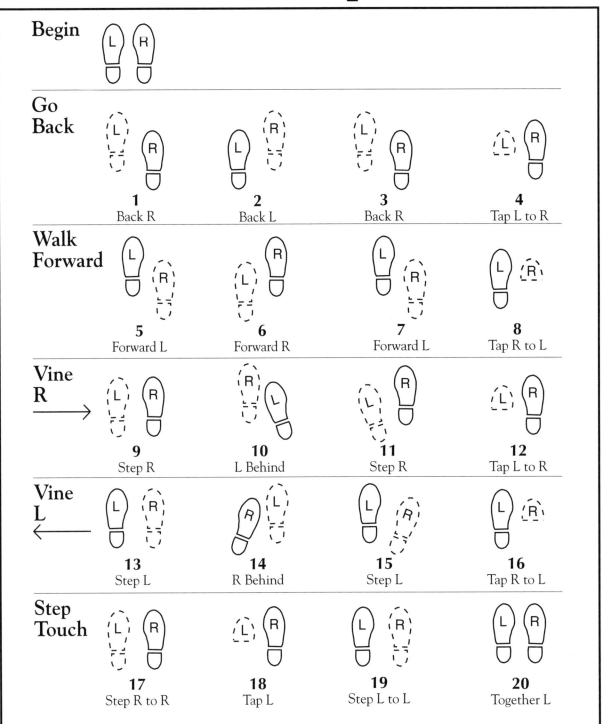

Begin

Go Back

1	2	3	4
Back R	Back L	Back R	Tap L to R

Walk Forward

5	6	7	8
Forward L	Forward R	Forward L	Tap R to L

Vine R →

9	10	11	12
Step R	L Behind	Step R	Tap L to R

Vine L ←

13	14	15	16
Step L	R Behind	Step L	Tap R to L

Step Touch

17	18	19	20
Step R to R	Tap L	Step L to L	Together L

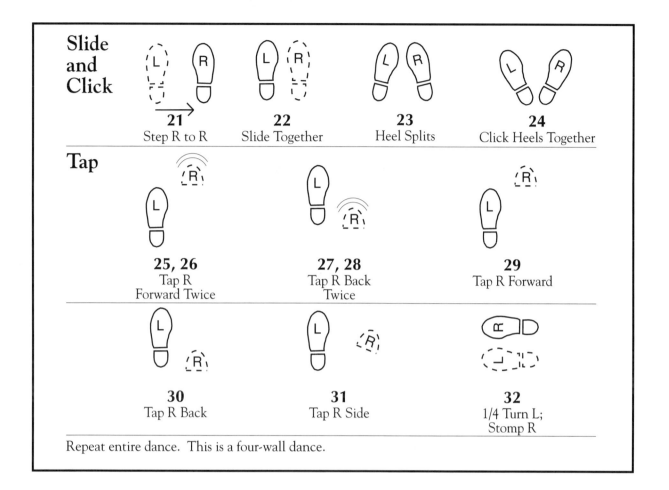

Slide and Click

21 Step R to R

22 Slide Together

23 Heel Splits

24 Click Heels Together

Tap

25, 26 Tap R Forward Twice

27, 28 Tap R Back Twice

29 Tap R Forward

30 Tap R Back

31 Tap R Side

32 1/4 Turn L; Stomp R

Repeat entire dance. This is a four-wall dance.

Cowboy Boogie

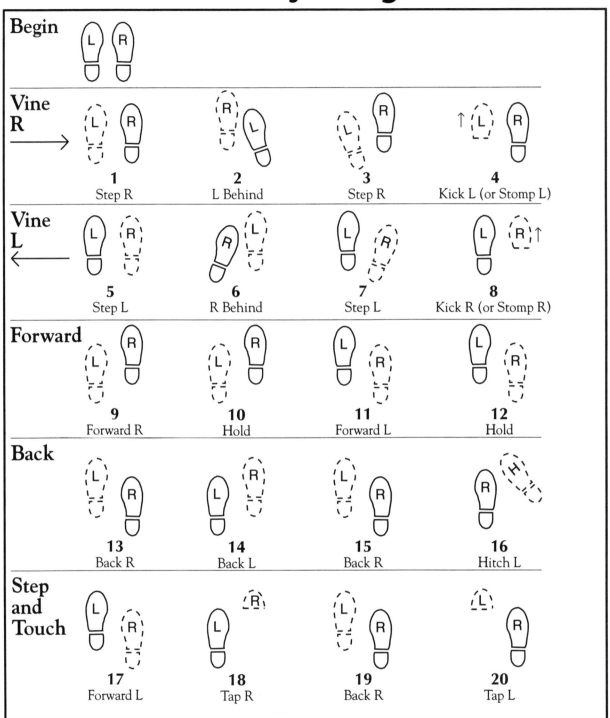

Begin

Vine R →

| 1 | 2 | 3 | 4 |
| Step R | L Behind | Step R | Kick L (or Stomp L) |

Vine L ←

| 5 | 6 | 7 | 8 |
| Step L | R Behind | Step L | Kick R (or Stomp R) |

Forward

| 9 | 10 | 11 | 12 |
| Forward R | Hold | Forward L | Hold |

Back

| 13 | 14 | 15 | 16 |
| Back R | Back L | Back R | Hitch L |

Step and Touch

| 17 | 18 | 19 | 20 |
| Forward L | Tap R | Back R | Tap L |

Rock

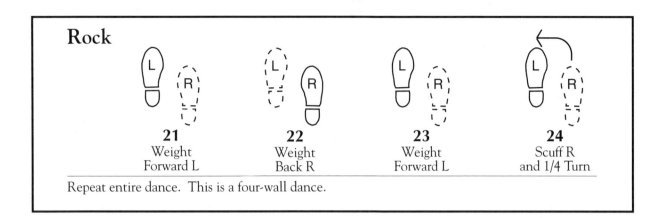

21
Weight
Forward L

22
Weight
Back R

23
Weight
Forward L

24
Scuff R
and 1/4 Turn

Repeat entire dance. This is a four-wall dance.

Cowboy Hustle

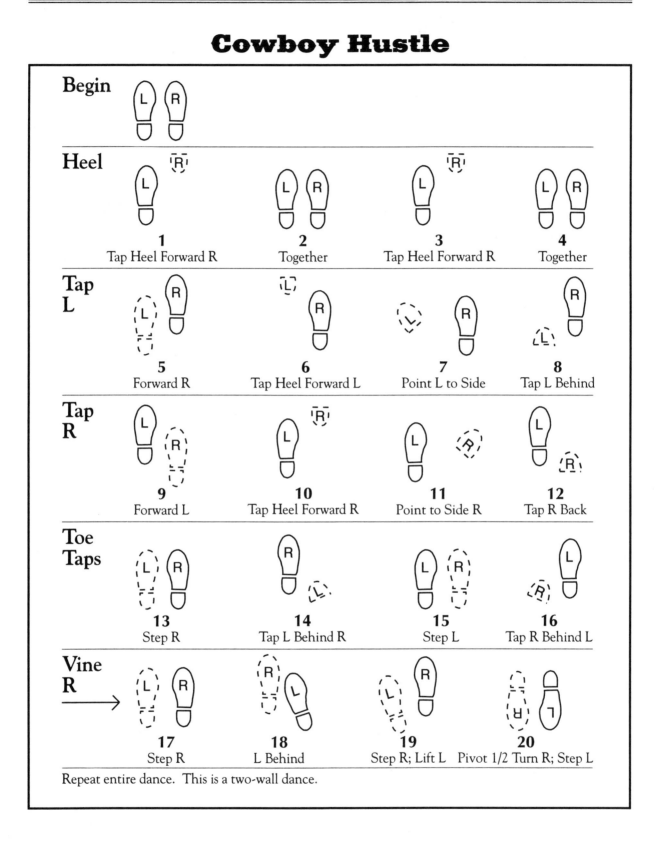

Begin

Heel

1 Tap Heel Forward R
2 Together
3 Tap Heel Forward R
4 Together

Tap L

5 Forward R
6 Tap Heel Forward L
7 Point L to Side
8 Tap L Behind

Tap R

9 Forward L
10 Tap Heel Forward R
11 Point to Side R
12 Tap R Back

Toe Taps

13 Step R
14 Tap L Behind R
15 Step L
16 Tap R Behind L

Vine R →

17 Step R
18 L Behind
19 Step R; Lift L
20 Pivot 1/2 Turn R; Step L

Repeat entire dance. This is a two-wall dance.

Double Dutch Bus

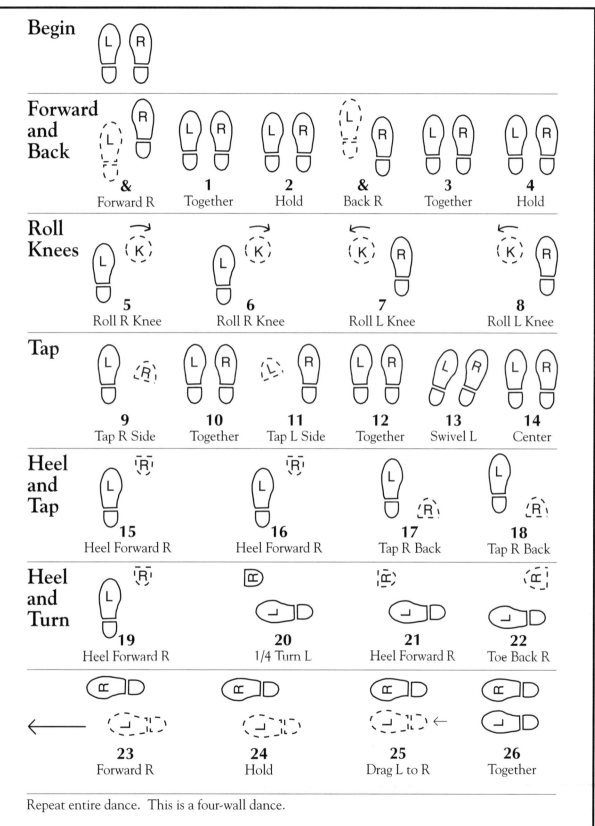

Begin

Forward and Back

&	1	2	&	3	4
Forward R	Together	Hold	Back R	Together	Hold

Roll Knees

5	6	7	8
Roll R Knee	Roll R Knee	Roll L Knee	Roll L Knee

Tap

9	10	11	12	13	14
Tap R Side	Together	Tap L Side	Together	Swivel L	Center

Heel and Tap

15	16	17	18
Heel Forward R	Heel Forward R	Tap R Back	Tap R Back

Heel and Turn

19	20	21	22
Heel Forward R	1/4 Turn L	Heel Forward R	Toe Back R

23	24	25	26
Forward R	Hold	Drag L to R	Together

Repeat entire dance. This is a four-wall dance.

Electric Slide

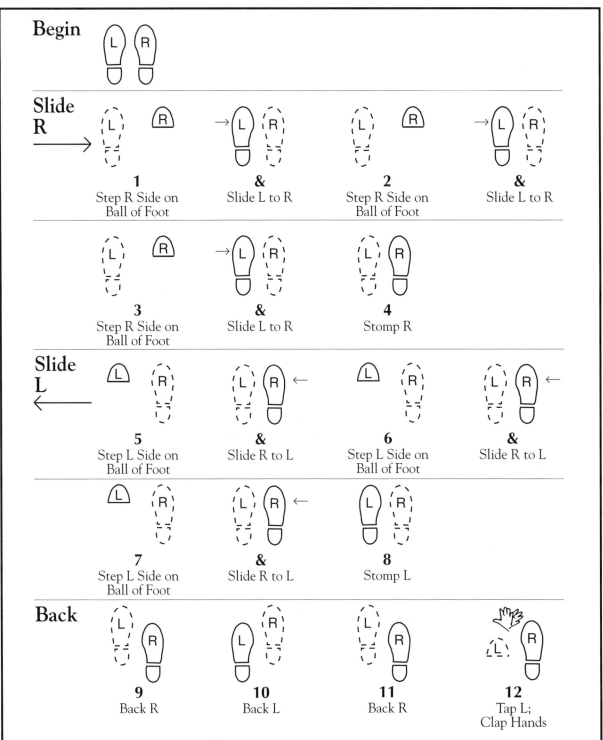

Begin

Slide R →

1	&	2	&
Step R Side on Ball of Foot	Slide L to R	Step R Side on Ball of Foot	Slide L to R

3	&	4
Step R Side on Ball of Foot	Slide L to R	Stomp R

Slide L ←

5	&	6	&
Step L Side on Ball of Foot	Slide R to L	Step L Side on Ball of Foot	Slide R to L

7	&	8
Step L Side on Ball of Foot	Slide R to L	Stomp L

Back

9	10	11	12
Back R	Back L	Back R	Tap L; Clap Hands

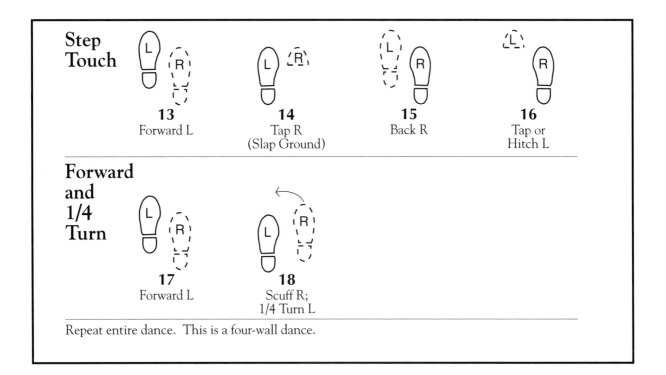

Step Touch

13
Forward L

14
Tap R
(Slap Ground)

15
Back R

16
Tap or
Hitch L

Forward and 1/4 Turn

17
Forward L

18
Scuff R;
1/4 Turn L

Repeat entire dance. This is a four-wall dance.

Electric Slide II

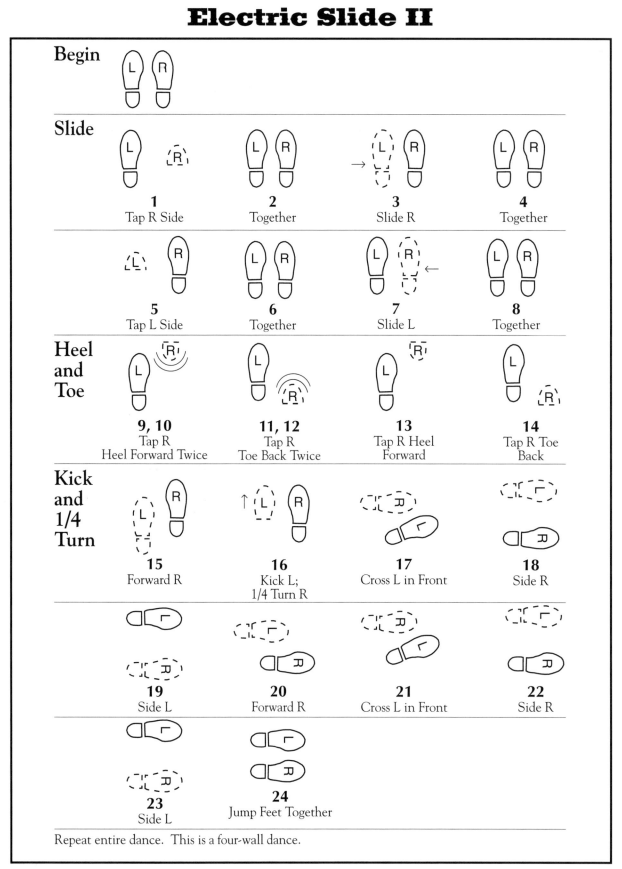

Begin

Slide

1
Tap R Side

2
Together

3
Slide R

4
Together

5
Tap L Side

6
Together

7
Slide L

8
Together

Heel and Toe

9, 10
Tap R
Heel Forward Twice

11, 12
Tap R
Toe Back Twice

13
Tap R Heel
Forward

14
Tap R Toe
Back

Kick and 1/4 Turn

15
Forward R

16
Kick L;
1/4 Turn R

17
Cross L in Front

18
Side R

19
Side L

20
Forward R

21
Cross L in Front

22
Side R

23
Side L

24
Jump Feet Together

Repeat entire dance. This is a four-wall dance.

Flying Eight

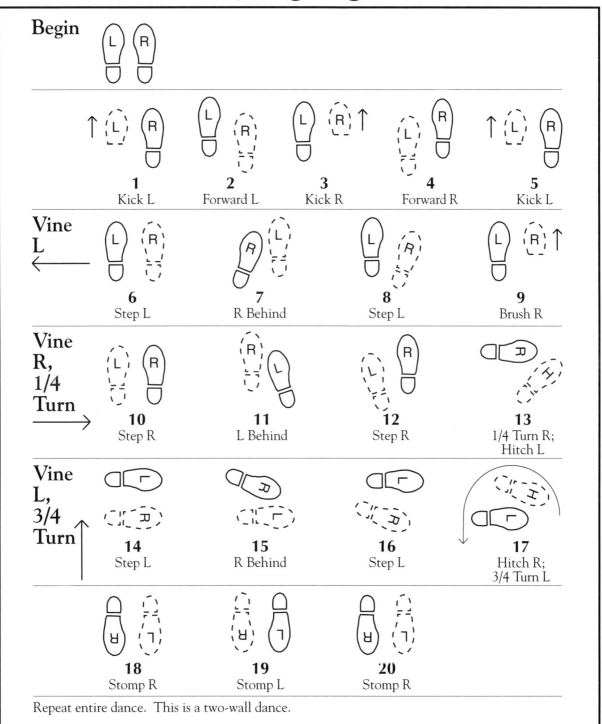

Begin

1 — Kick L
2 — Forward L
3 — Kick R
4 — Forward R
5 — Kick L

Vine L
6 — Step L
7 — R Behind
8 — Step L
9 — Brush R

Vine R, 1/4 Turn
10 — Step R
11 — L Behind
12 — Step R
13 — 1/4 Turn R; Hitch L

Vine L, 3/4 Turn
14 — Step L
15 — R Behind
16 — Step L
17 — Hitch R; 3/4 Turn L

18 — Stomp R
19 — Stomp L
20 — Stomp R

Repeat entire dance. This is a two-wall dance.

Freeze

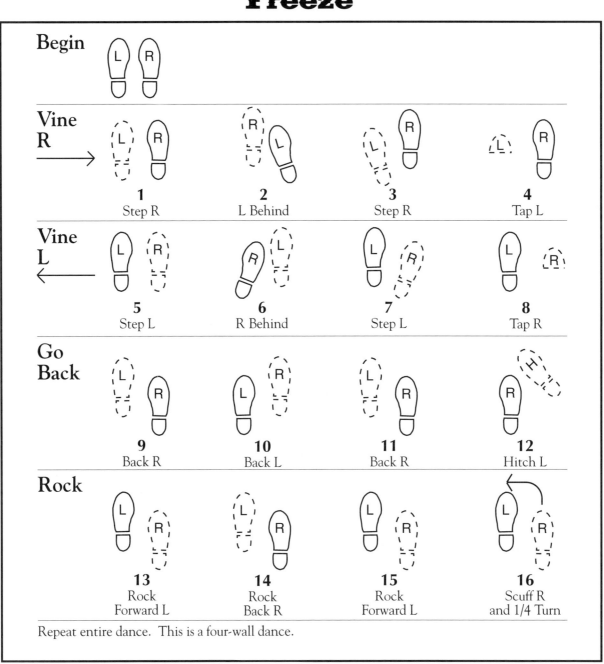

Begin

Vine R →

1	2	3	4
Step R	L Behind	Step R	Tap L

Vine L ←

5	6	7	8
Step L	R Behind	Step L	Tap R

Go Back

9	10	11	12
Back R	Back L	Back R	Hitch L

Rock

13	14	15	16
Rock Forward L	Rock Back R	Rock Forward L	Scuff R and 1/4 Turn

Repeat entire dance. This is a four-wall dance.

Freeze II

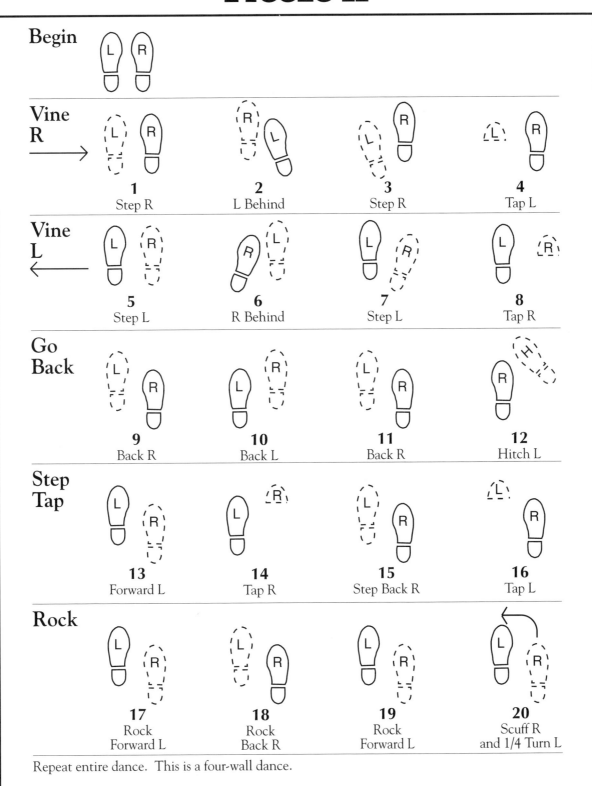

	1	2	3	4
Begin				
Vine R →	Step R	L Behind	Step R	Tap L

	5	6	7	8
Vine L ←	Step L	R Behind	Step L	Tap R

	9	10	11	12
Go Back	Back R	Back L	Back R	Hitch L

	13	14	15	16
Step Tap	Forward L	Tap R	Step Back R	Tap L

	17	18	19	20
Rock	Rock Forward L	Rock Back R	Rock Forward L	Scuff R and 1/4 Turn L

Repeat entire dance. This is a four-wall dance.

Hitch-Hiker

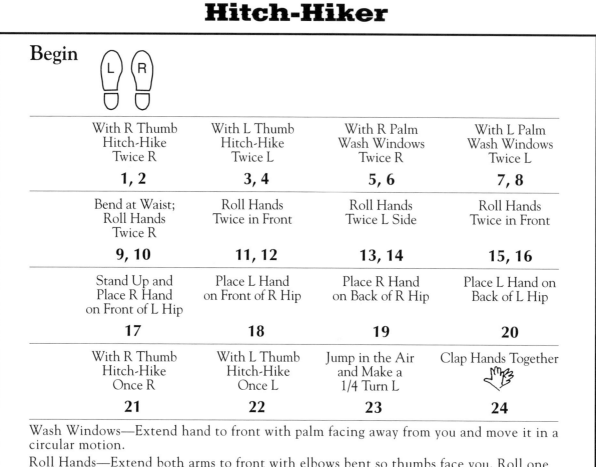

Begin

With R Thumb Hitch-Hike Twice R	With L Thumb Hitch-Hike Twice L	With R Palm Wash Windows Twice R	With L Palm Wash Windows Twice L
1, 2	**3, 4**	**5, 6**	**7, 8**
Bend at Waist; Roll Hands Twice R	Roll Hands Twice in Front	Roll Hands Twice L Side	Roll Hands Twice in Front
9, 10	**11, 12**	**13, 14**	**15, 16**
Stand Up and Place R Hand on Front of L Hip	Place L Hand on Front of R Hip	Place R Hand on Back of R Hip	Place L Hand on Back of L Hip
17	**18**	**19**	**20**
With R Thumb Hitch-Hike Once R	With L Thumb Hitch-Hike Once L	Jump in the Air and Make a 1/4 Turn L	Clap Hands Together
21	**22**	**23**	**24**

Wash Windows—Extend hand to front with palm facing away from you and move it in a circular motion.

Roll Hands—Extend both arms to front with elbows bent so thumbs face you. Roll one hand over the other in a circular motion.

Repeat entire dance. This is a four-wall dance.

Tennessee Stroll

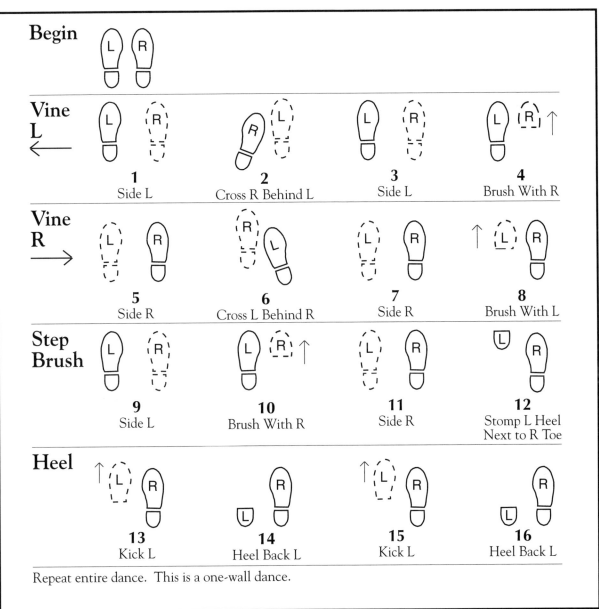

Begin

Vine L ←
1 — Side L
2 — Cross R Behind L
3 — Side L
4 — Brush With R

Vine R →
5 — Side R
6 — Cross L Behind R
7 — Side R
8 — Brush With L

Step Brush
9 — Side L
10 — Brush With R
11 — Side R
12 — Stomp L Heel Next to R Toe

Heel
13 — Kick L
14 — Heel Back L
15 — Kick L
16 — Heel Back L

Repeat entire dance. This is a one-wall dance.

Hooked on Country

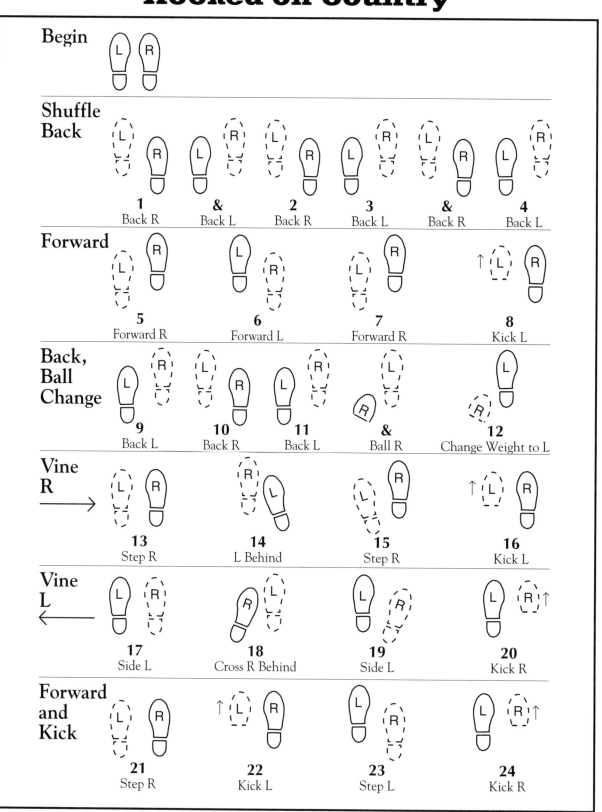

Begin	L R				
Shuffle Back	**1** Back R	**&** Back L	**2** Back R	**3** Back L	**&** Back R	**4** Back L
Forward	**5** Forward R	**6** Forward L	**7** Forward R	**8** Kick L
Back, Ball Change	**9** Back L	**10** Back R	**11** Back L	**&** Ball R	**12** Change Weight to L
Vine R →	**13** Step R	**14** L Behind	**15** Step R	**16** Kick L
Vine L ←	**17** Side L	**18** Cross R Behind	**19** Side L	**20** Kick R
Forward and Kick	**21** Step R	**22** Kick L	**23** Step L	**24** Kick R

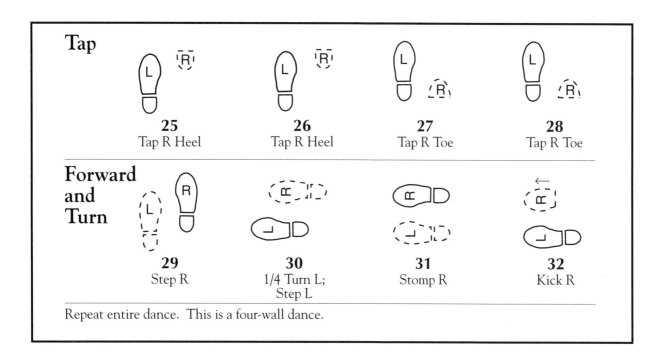

Tap

25
Tap R Heel

26
Tap R Heel

27
Tap R Toe

28
Tap R Toe

Forward and Turn

29
Step R

30
1/4 Turn L;
Step L

31
Stomp R

32
Kick R

Repeat entire dance. This is a four-wall dance.

Reggae Cowboy

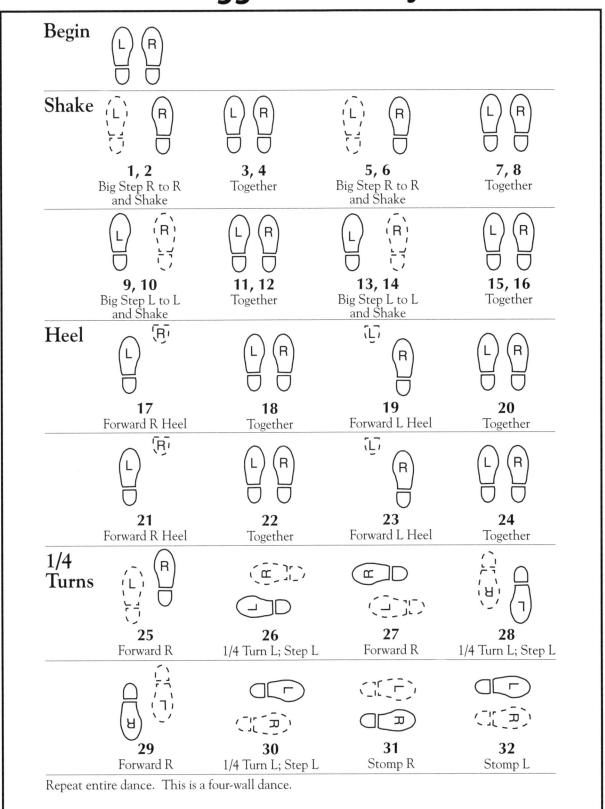

Begin

Shake

1, 2
Big Step R to R
and Shake

3, 4
Together

5, 6
Big Step R to R
and Shake

7, 8
Together

9, 10
Big Step L to L
and Shake

11, 12
Together

13, 14
Big Step L to L
and Shake

15, 16
Together

Heel

17
Forward R Heel

18
Together

19
Forward L Heel

20
Together

21
Forward R Heel

22
Together

23
Forward L Heel

24
Together

1/4 Turns

25
Forward R

26
1/4 Turn L; Step L

27
Forward R

28
1/4 Turn L; Step L

29
Forward R

30
1/4 Turn L; Step L

31
Stomp R

32
Stomp L

Repeat entire dance. This is a four-wall dance.

Reggae Cowboy II

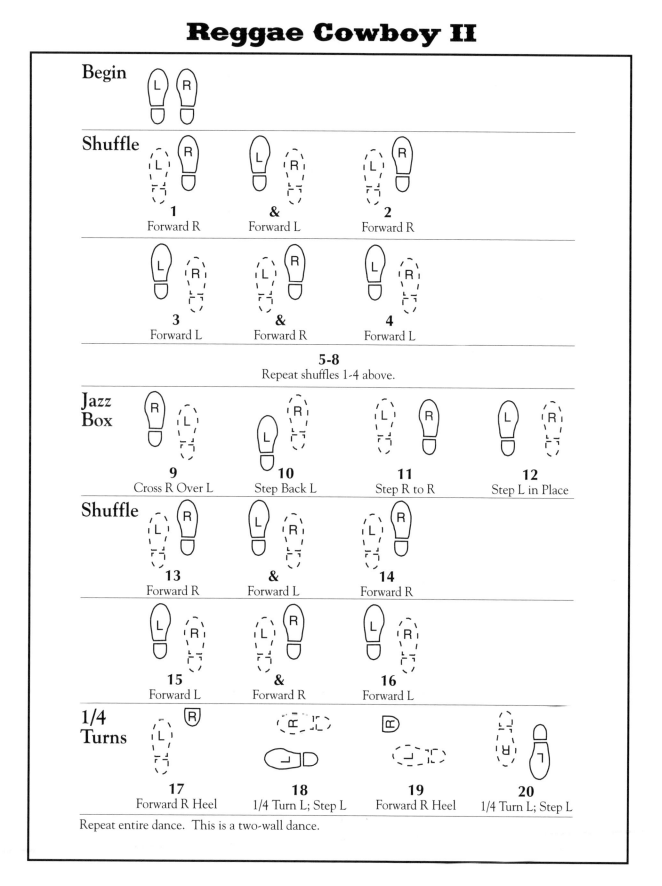

Begin

Shuffle

1 Forward R   **&** Forward L   **2** Forward R

3 Forward L   **&** Forward R   **4** Forward L

5-8 Repeat shuffles 1-4 above.

Jazz Box

9 Cross R Over L   **10** Step Back L   **11** Step R to R   **12** Step L in Place

Shuffle

13 Forward R   **&** Forward L   **14** Forward R

15 Forward L   **&** Forward R   **16** Forward L

1/4 Turns

17 Forward R Heel   **18** 1/4 Turn L; Step L   **19** Forward R Heel   **20** 1/4 Turn L; Step L

Repeat entire dance. This is a two-wall dance.

Sleazy Slide

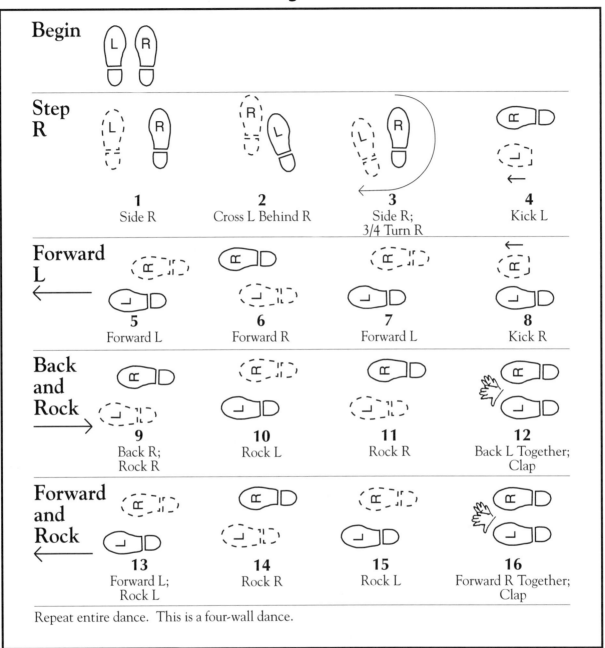

1 Side R	**2** Cross L Behind R	**3** Side R; 3/4 Turn R	**4** Kick L
5 Forward L	**6** Forward R	**7** Forward L	**8** Kick R
9 Back R; Rock R	**10** Rock L	**11** Rock R	**12** Back L Together; Clap
13 Forward L; Rock L	**14** Rock R	**15** Rock L	**16** Forward R Together; Clap

Repeat entire dance. This is a four-wall dance.

Traveling Four Corners

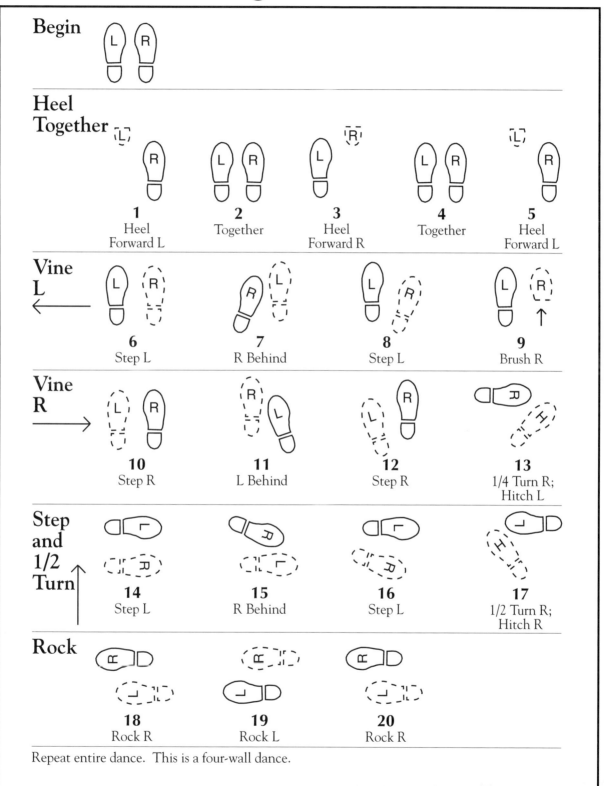

Begin

Heel Together

1
Heel
Forward L

2
Together

3
Heel
Forward R

4
Together

5
Heel
Forward L

Vine L

6
Step L

7
R Behind

8
Step L

9
Brush R

Vine R

10
Step R

11
L Behind

12
Step R

13
1/4 Turn R;
Hitch L

Step and 1/2 Turn

14
Step L

15
R Behind

16
Step L

17
1/2 Turn R;
Hitch R

Rock

18
Rock R

19
Rock L

20
Rock R

Repeat entire dance. This is a four-wall dance.

CHAPTER 4

A Little Harder, But a Lot More Fun!

Intermediate Line Dances

Congratulations for making it this far! You should be proud of yourself. With your motivation you won't have any problem tackling more advanced dances. We're going to increase the tempo a bit and add some fancier footwork as you learn combination steps like the cha-cha, shuffles, scoots, and slides. The dances in this chapter have more counts than the ones in the previous chapter and incorporate more flair and style in turns and changes of direction. Some of the more intricate moves require two steps to one beat of music, but don't feel intimidated—I know you can do it! Are you ready? We're going to have some fun now!

Amos Moses

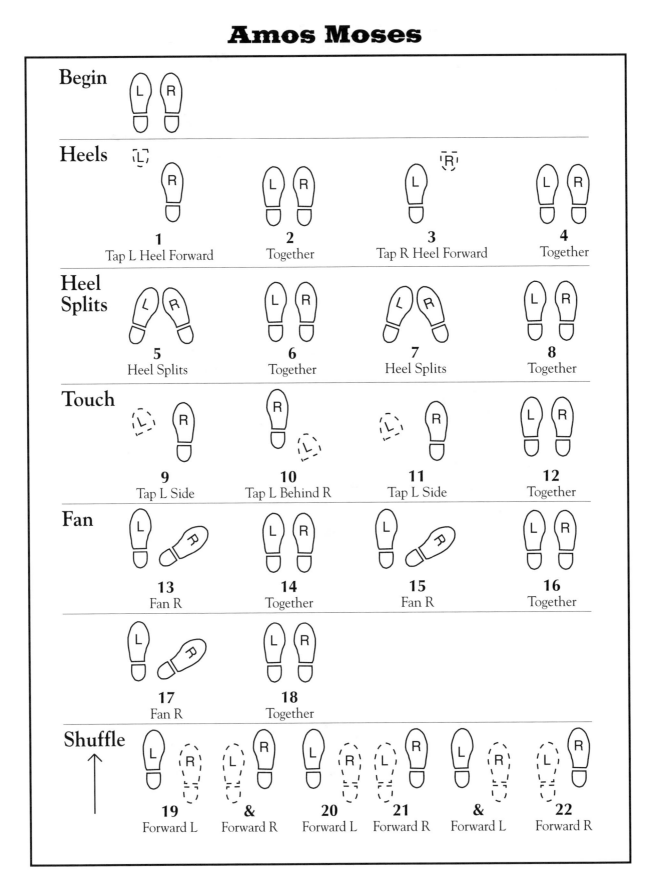

Begin

Heels

1 Tap L Heel Forward

2 Together

3 Tap R Heel Forward

4 Together

Heel Splits

5 Heel Splits

6 Together

7 Heel Splits

8 Together

Touch

9 Tap L Side

10 Tap L Behind R

11 Tap L Side

12 Together

Fan

13 Fan R

14 Together

15 Fan R

16 Together

17 Fan R

18 Together

Shuffle

19 Forward L

& Forward R

20 Forward L

21 Forward R

& Forward L

22 Forward R

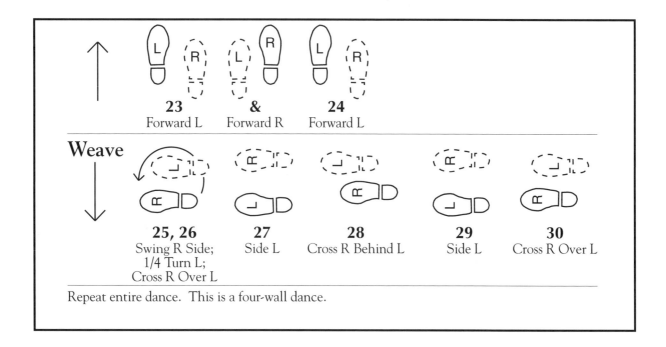

23
Forward L

&
Forward R

24
Forward L

Weave

25, 26
Swing R Side;
1/4 Turn L;
Cross R Over L

27
Side L

28
Cross R Behind L

29
Side L

30
Cross R Over L

Repeat entire dance. This is a four-wall dance.

Black Velvet

(Also known as "Ski Bumpus")

Begin

Shuffle

1	&	2	3	&	4
Forward R	Forward L	Forward R	Forward L	Forward R	Forward L

1/2 Turn

5	6
Forward R; 1/2 Turn L	Step L

Shuffle

7	&	8	9	&	10
Forward R	Forward L	Forward R	Forward L	Forward R	Forward L

1/2 Turn

11	12
Forward R; 1/2 Turn L	Step L

Jazz Box

13	14	15	16
Cross R Over L	Back L	Side R	Stomp L to R

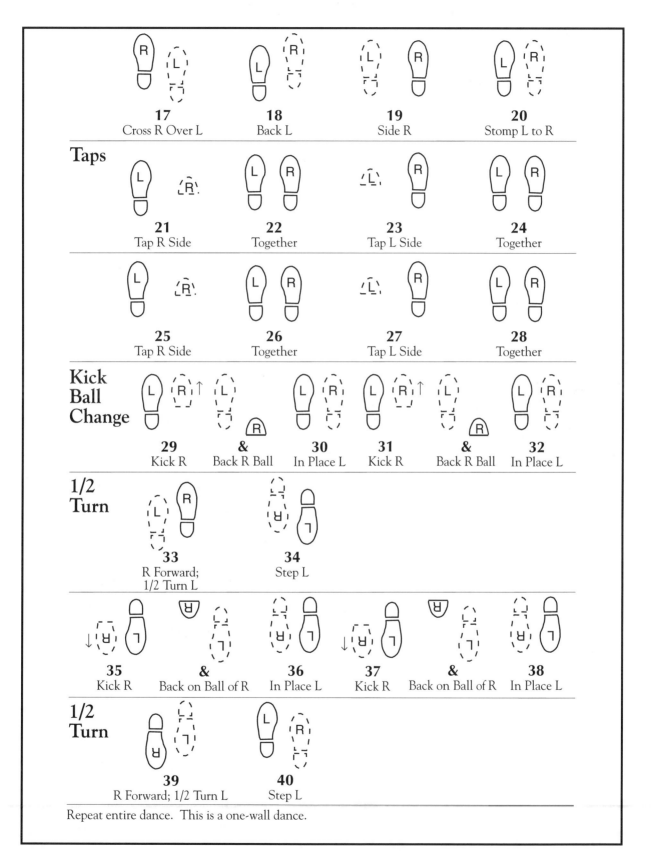

17
Cross R Over L

18
Back L

19
Side R

20
Stomp L to R

Taps

21
Tap R Side

22
Together

23
Tap L Side

24
Together

25
Tap R Side

26
Together

27
Tap L Side

28
Together

Kick Ball Change

29
Kick R

&
Back R Ball

30
In Place L

31
Kick R

&
Back R Ball

32
In Place L

1/2 Turn

33
R Forward;
1/2 Turn L

34
Step L

35
Kick R

&
Back on Ball of R

36
In Place L

37
Kick R

&
Back on Ball of R

38
In Place L

1/2 Turn

39
R Forward; 1/2 Turn L

40
Step L

Repeat entire dance. This is a one-wall dance.

Boot Scoot Boogie

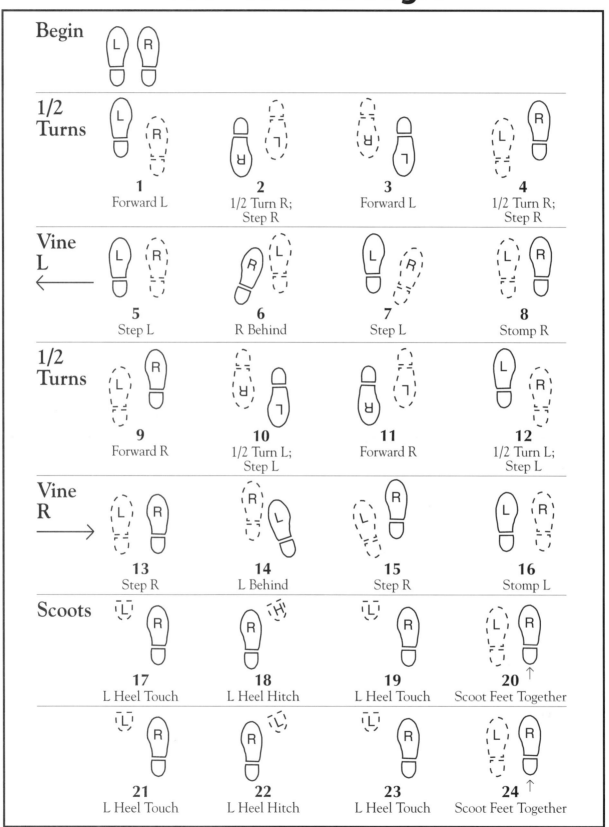

Begin			
1/2 Turns			
1 Forward L	**2** 1/2 Turn R; Step R	**3** Forward L	**4** 1/2 Turn R; Step R
Vine L ←			
5 Step L	**6** R Behind	**7** Step L	**8** Stomp R
1/2 Turns			
9 Forward R	**10** 1/2 Turn L; Step L	**11** Forward R	**12** 1/2 Turn L; Step L
Vine R →			
13 Step R	**14** L Behind	**15** Step R	**16** Stomp L
Scoots			
17 L Heel Touch	**18** L Heel Hitch	**19** L Heel Touch	**20** Scoot Feet Together
21 L Heel Touch	**22** L Heel Hitch	**23** L Heel Touch	**24** Scoot Feet Together

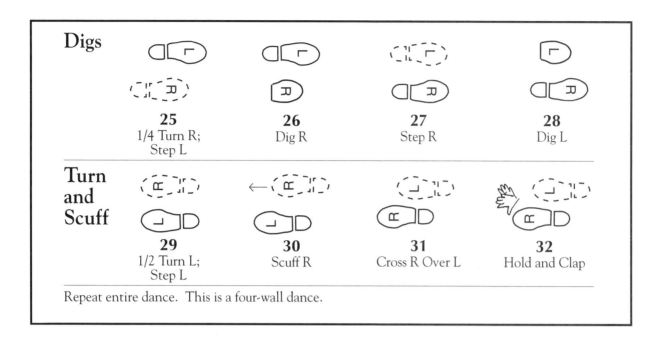

Digs

25	26	27	28
1/4 Turn R; Step L	Dig R	Step R	Dig L

Turn and Scuff

29	30	31	32
1/2 Turn L; Step L	Scuff R	Cross R Over L	Hold and Clap

Repeat entire dance. This is a four-wall dance.

Clyde

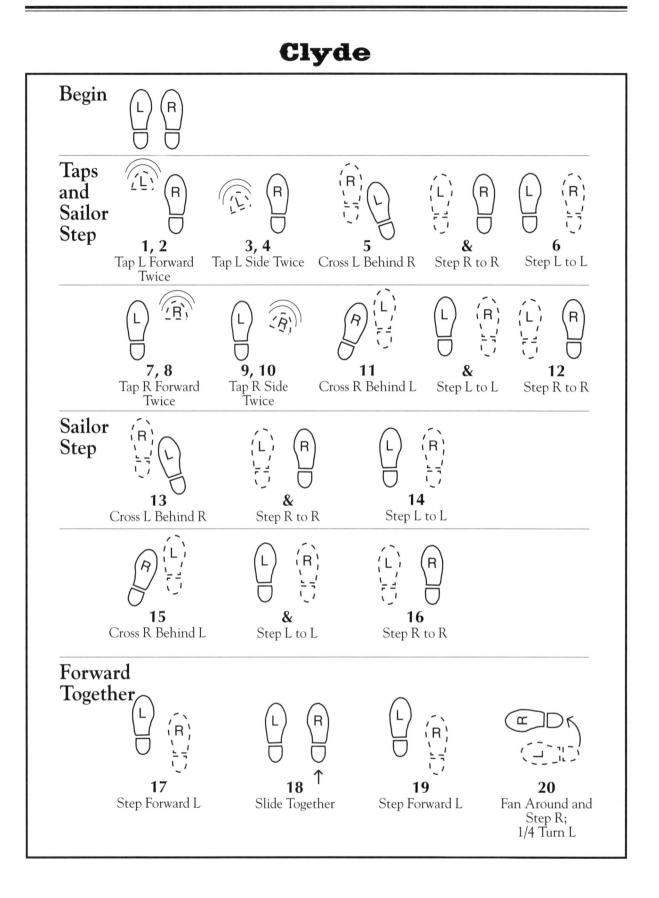

Begin

Taps and Sailor Step

1, 2 Tap L Forward Twice

3, 4 Tap L Side Twice

5 Cross L Behind R

& Step R to R

6 Step L to L

7, 8 Tap R Forward Twice

9, 10 Tap R Side Twice

11 Cross R Behind L

& Step L to L

12 Step R to R

Sailor Step

13 Cross L Behind R

& Step R to R

14 Step L to L

15 Cross R Behind L

& Step L to L

16 Step R to R

Forward Together

17 Step Forward L

18 Slide Together

19 Step Forward L

20 Fan Around and Step R; 1/4 Turn L

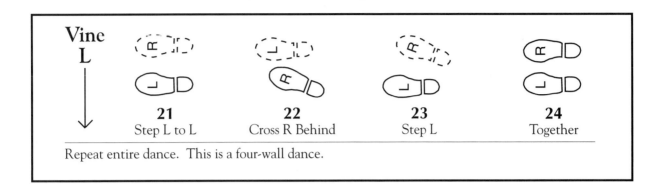

Vine
L

21
Step L to L

22
Cross R Behind

23
Step L

24
Together

Repeat entire dance. This is a four-wall dance.

Country Strut

Begin

Heel, Hook

1	2	3	4
R Heel Forward	Hook R Over L	R Heel Forward	Toe Side R

5	6	7	8
R Heel Forward	Together	L Heel Forward	Hook L Over R

9	10	11	12
L Heel Forward	Toe Side L	L Heel Forward	Toe Back L

Forward Kick

13	14	15	16
Forward L	Kick R	Back R	Toe Back L

Vine 1/2 Turn

17	18	19	20
Side L	Cross R Behind L	Side L; 1/2 Turn L	Brush Heel R

Heel, Step

21	22	23	24
R Heel Forward	Step R	L Heel Forward	Step L

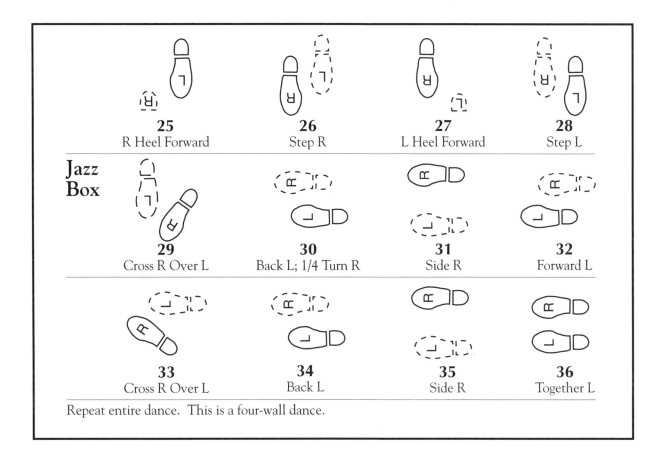

25
R Heel Forward

26
Step R

27
L Heel Forward

28
Step L

Jazz Box

29
Cross R Over L

30
Back L; 1/4 Turn R

31
Side R

32
Forward L

33
Cross R Over L

34
Back L

35
Side R

36
Together L

Repeat entire dance. This is a four-wall dance.

Cowboy Cha-Cha

Begin	L R				

Cha-Cha	**1** Forward L	**2** Back R	**3** Back L	**&** Back R	**4** Back L

Cha-Cha With Turn	**5** Back R	**6** Forward L	**7** Forward R; Begin 1/2 Turn L	**&** Back L	**8** Back R

	9 Back L	**10** Forward R	**11** Forward L; Begin 1/2 Turn R	**&** Back R	**12** Back L

1/4 Turn	**13** Back R	**14** Forward L	**15** Forward R; Begin 1/4 Turn L	**&** Step L Together	**16** Step R to R

1/2 Turn	**17** Forward L	**18** 1/2 Turn R; Step R	**19** Forward L	**20** 1/2 Turn R; Step R

Repeat entire dance. This is a four-wall dance.

Stray Cat Strut

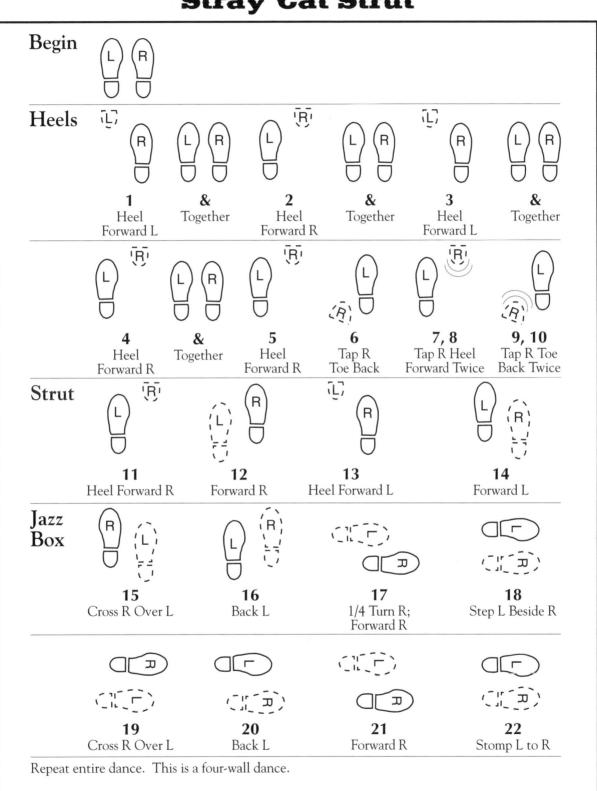

Begin

Heels

1	&	2	&	3	&
Heel Forward L	Together	Heel Forward R	Together	Heel Forward L	Together

4	&	5	6	7, 8	9, 10
Heel Forward R	Together	Heel Forward R	Tap R Toe Back	Tap R Heel Forward Twice	Tap R Toe Back Twice

Strut

11	12	13	14
Heel Forward R	Forward R	Heel Forward L	Forward L

Jazz Box

15	16	17	18
Cross R Over L	Back L	1/4 Turn R; Forward R	Step L Beside R

19	20	21	22
Cross R Over L	Back L	Forward R	Stomp L to R

Repeat entire dance. This is a four-wall dance.

Cowboy Hip-Hop

Begin

Running Man

1	**&**	**2**	**&**
Step R	Slide R Back	Step L	Slide L Back

3	**&**	**4**
Step R	Slide R Back	Step L Forward

Hips

5	**6**	**7**	**8**
Step R as Hips Roll Forward	Hips Roll Back	Hips Roll Forward	Hips Roll Back

Electric Kick

9	**10**	**11**	**12**
Jump Back R; Kick L	L Forward	Jump R Forward	L Back

Electric Kick Double Time

13	**&**	**14**	**&**
Jump Back R; Kick L	L Forward	Jump R Forward	L Back

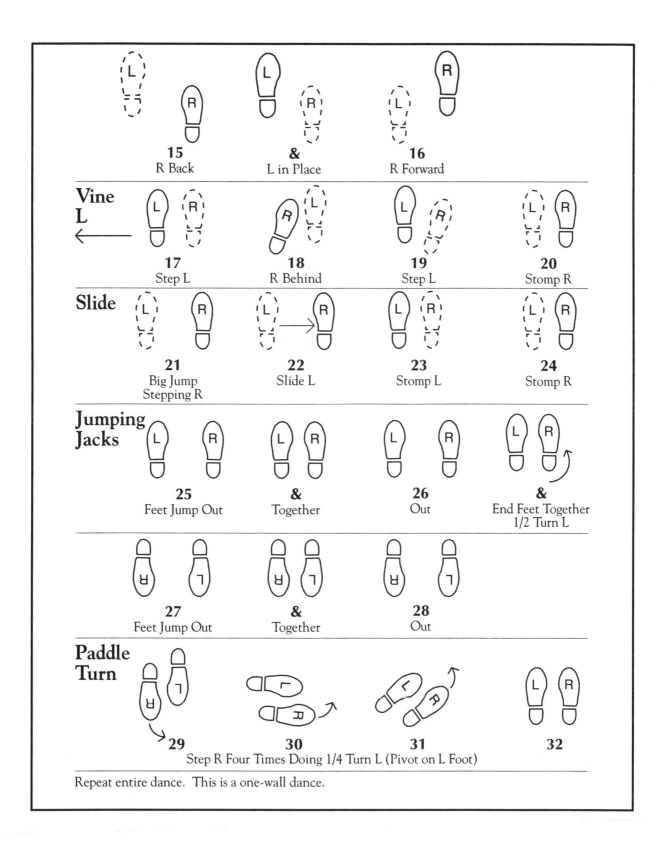

15
R Back

&
L in Place

16
R Forward

Vine L

17
Step L

18
R Behind

19
Step L

20
Stomp R

Slide

21
Big Jump
Stepping R

22
Slide L

23
Stomp L

24
Stomp R

Jumping Jacks

25
Feet Jump Out

&
Together

26
Out

&
End Feet Together
1/2 Turn L

27
Feet Jump Out

&
Together

28
Out

Paddle Turn

29

30

31

32

Step R Four Times Doing 1/4 Turn L (Pivot on L Foot)

Repeat entire dance. This is a one-wall dance.

Crazy 8's

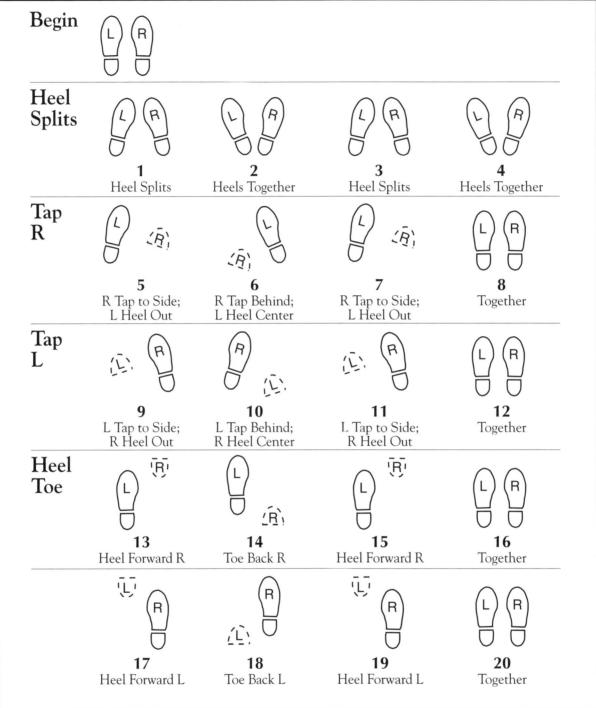

Begin				
Heel Splits	**1** Heel Splits	**2** Heels Together	**3** Heel Splits	**4** Heels Together
Tap R	**5** R Tap to Side; L Heel Out	**6** R Tap Behind; L Heel Center	**7** R Tap to Side; L Heel Out	**8** Together
Tap L	**9** L Tap to Side; R Heel Out	**10** L Tap Behind; R Heel Center	**11** L Tap to Side; R Heel Out	**12** Together
Heel Toe	**13** Heel Forward R	**14** Toe Back R	**15** Heel Forward R	**16** Together
	17 Heel Forward L	**18** Toe Back L	**19** Heel Forward L	**20** Together

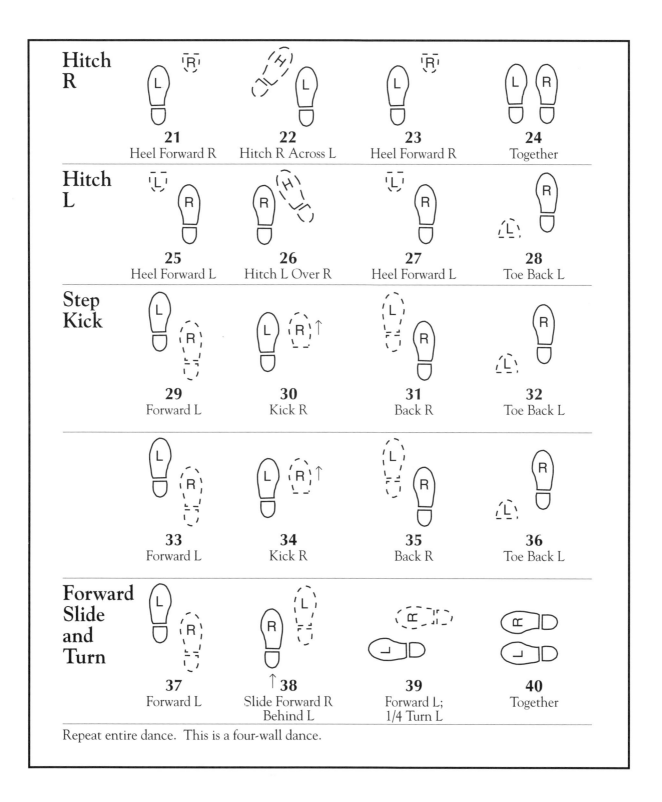

Hitch R

21 Heel Forward R

22 Hitch R Across L

23 Heel Forward R

24 Together

Hitch L

25 Heel Forward L

26 Hitch L Over R

27 Heel Forward L

28 Toe Back L

Step Kick

29 Forward L

30 Kick R

31 Back R

32 Toe Back L

33 Forward L

34 Kick R

35 Back R

36 Toe Back L

Forward Slide and Turn

37 Forward L

38 Slide Forward R Behind L

39 Forward L; 1/4 Turn L

40 Together

Repeat entire dance. This is a four-wall dance.

Dallas Shuffle

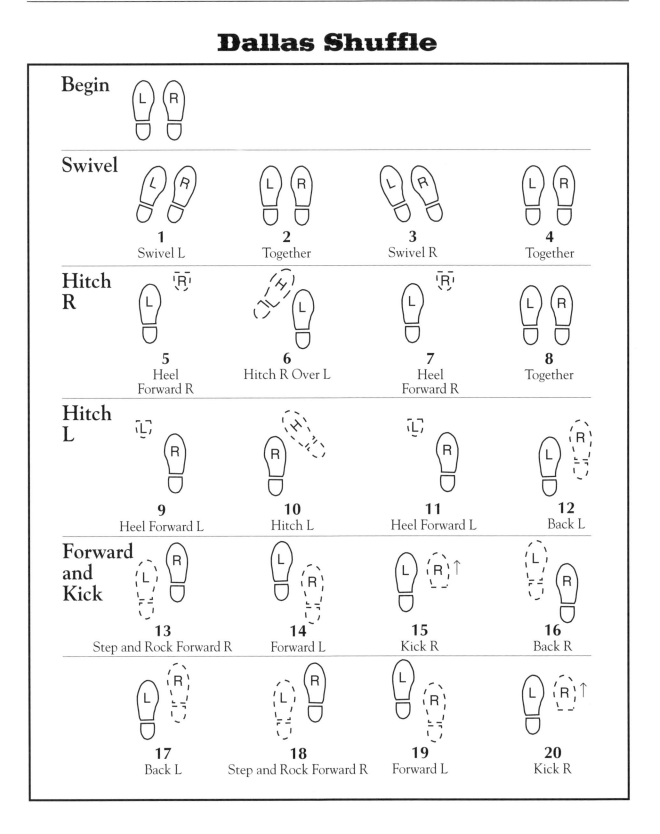

Begin

Swivel

1 — Swivel L
2 — Together
3 — Swivel R
4 — Together

Hitch R

5 — Heel Forward R
6 — Hitch R Over L
7 — Heel Forward R
8 — Together

Hitch L

9 — Heel Forward L
10 — Hitch L
11 — Heel Forward L
12 — Back L

Forward and Kick

13 — Step and Rock Forward R
14 — Forward L
15 — Kick R
16 — Back R

17 — Back L
18 — Step and Rock Forward R
19 — Forward L
20 — Kick R

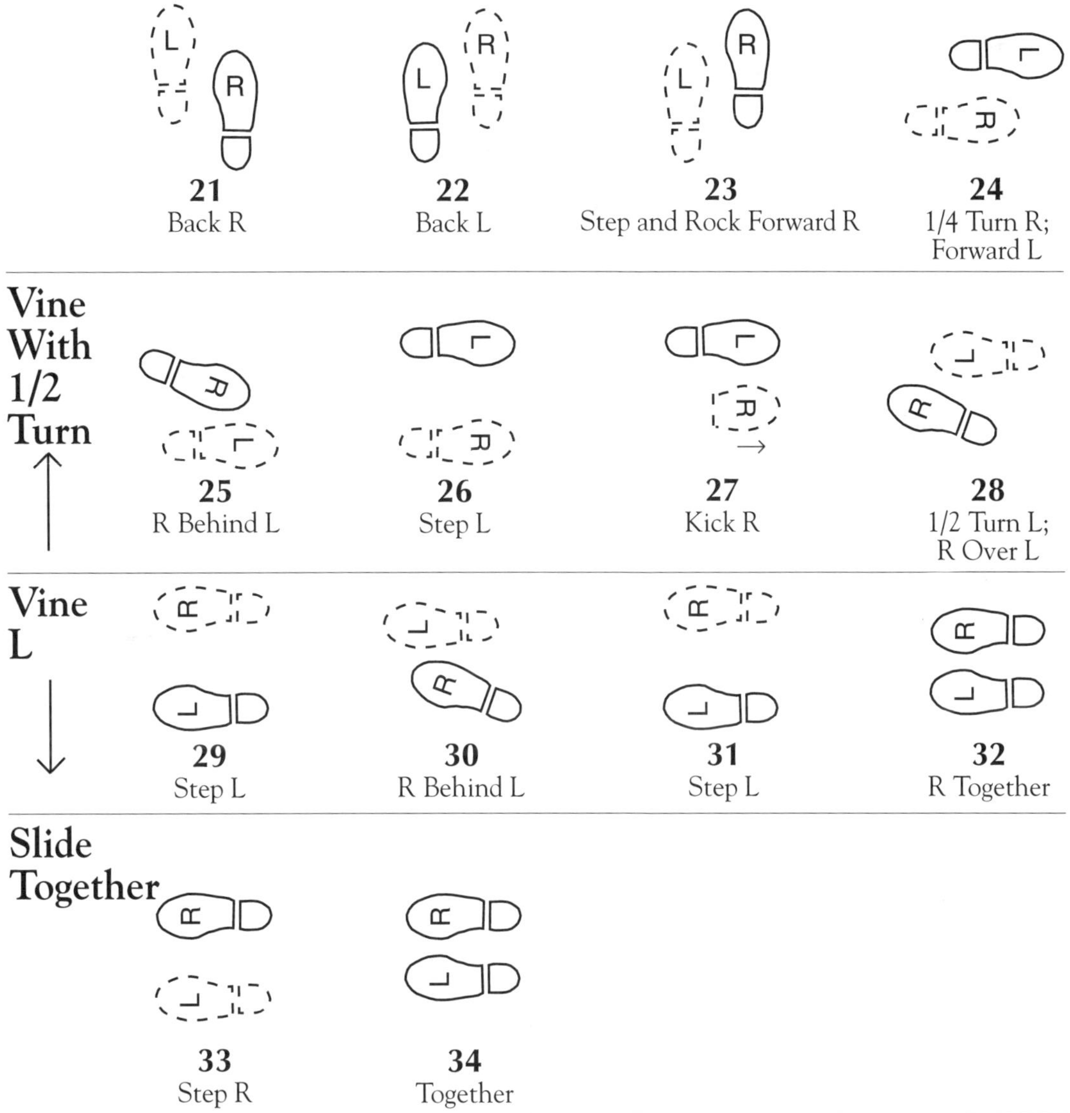

21
Back R

22
Back L

23
Step and Rock Forward R

24
1/4 Turn R;
Forward L

Vine With 1/2 Turn

25
R Behind L

26
Step L

27
Kick R

28
1/2 Turn L;
R Over L

Vine L

29
Step L

30
R Behind L

31
Step L

32
R Together

Slide Together

33
Step R

34
Together

Repeat entire dance. This is a four-wall dance.

Eight Corners

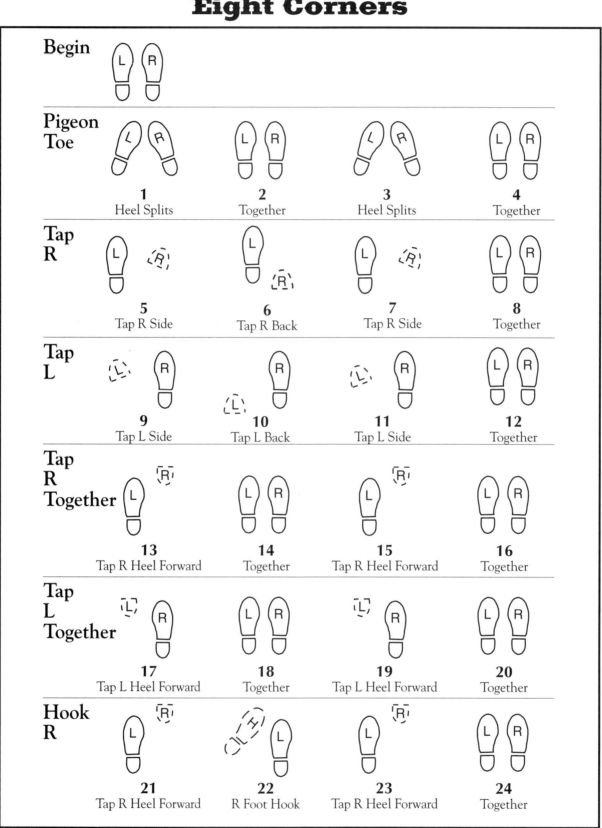

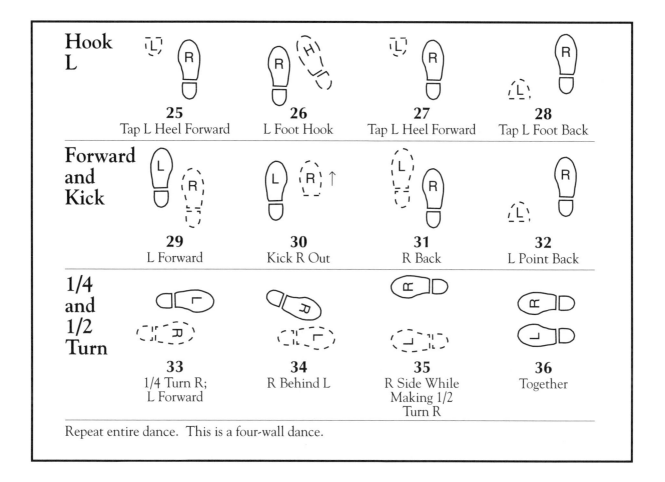

Hook L

25	26	27	28
Tap L Heel Forward	L Foot Hook	Tap L Heel Forward	Tap L Foot Back

Forward and Kick

29	30	31	32
L Forward	Kick R Out	R Back	L Point Back

1/4 and 1/2 Turn

33	34	35	36
1/4 Turn R; L Forward	R Behind L	R Side While Making 1/2 Turn R	Together

Repeat entire dance. This is a four-wall dance.

Elvira

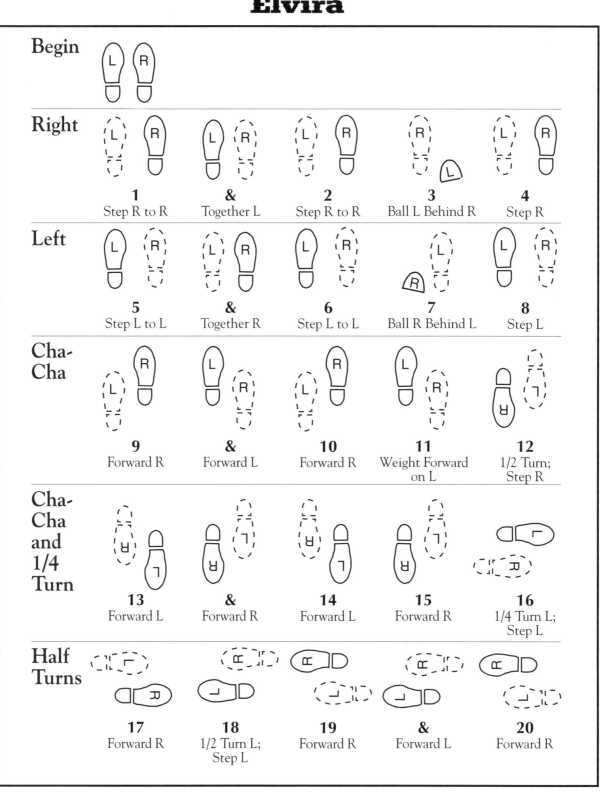

Begin					
Right	**1** Step R to R	**&** Together L	**2** Step R to R	**3** Ball L Behind R	**4** Step R
Left	**5** Step L to L	**&** Together R	**6** Step L to L	**7** Ball R Behind L	**8** Step L
Cha-Cha	**9** Forward R	**&** Forward L	**10** Forward R	**11** Weight Forward on L	**12** 1/2 Turn; Step R
Cha-Cha and 1/4 Turn	**13** Forward L	**&** Forward R	**14** Forward L	**15** Forward R	**16** 1/4 Turn L; Step L
Half Turns	**17** Forward R	**18** 1/2 Turn L; Step L	**19** Forward R	**&** Forward L	**20** Forward R

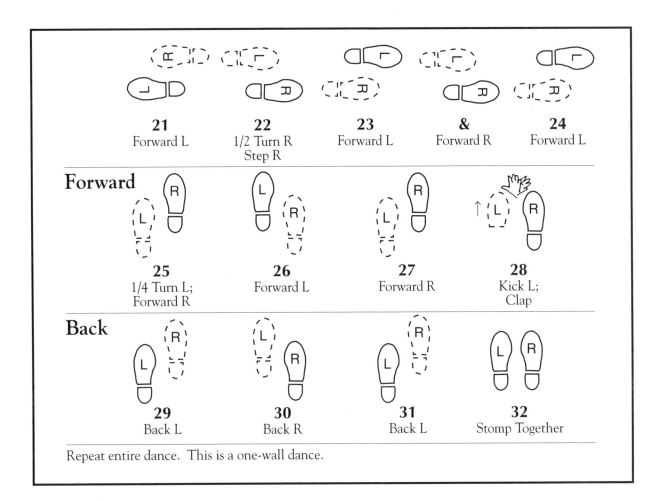

21
Forward L

22
1/2 Turn R
Step R

23
Forward L

&
Forward R

24
Forward L

Forward

25
1/4 Turn L;
Forward R

26
Forward L

27
Forward R

28
Kick L;
Clap

Back

29
Back L

30
Back R

31
Back L

32
Stomp Together

Repeat entire dance. This is a one-wall dance.

Funky Cowboy

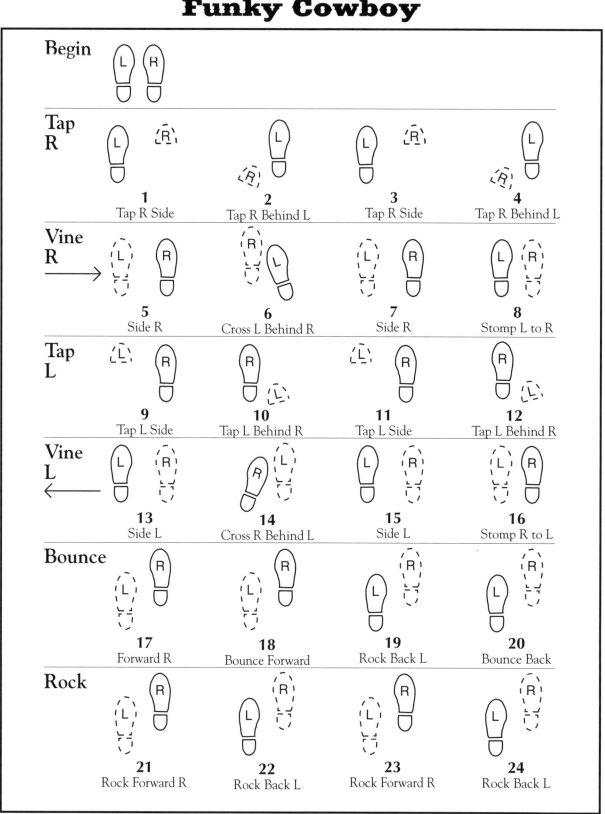

Begin

Tap R

1
Tap R Side

2
Tap R Behind L

3
Tap R Side

4
Tap R Behind L

Vine R →

5
Side R

6
Cross L Behind R

7
Side R

8
Stomp L to R

Tap L

9
Tap L Side

10
Tap L Behind R

11
Tap L Side

12
Tap L Behind R

Vine L ←

13
Side L

14
Cross R Behind L

15
Side L

16
Stomp R to L

Bounce

17
Forward R

18
Bounce Forward

19
Rock Back L

20
Bounce Back

Rock

21
Rock Forward R

22
Rock Back L

23
Rock Forward R

24
Rock Back L

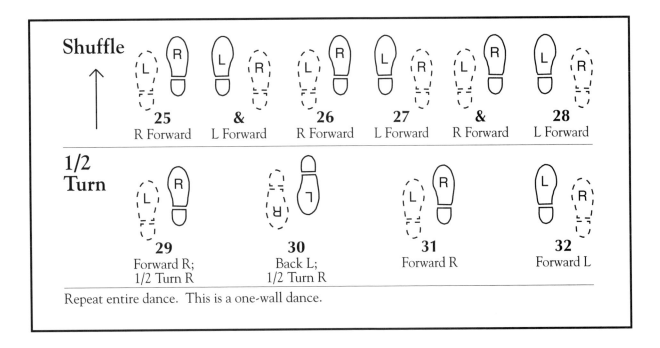

Shuffle

| **25** | **&** | **26** | **27** | **&** | **28** |
| R Forward | L Forward | R Forward | L Forward | R Forward | L Forward |

1/2 Turn

| **29** | **30** | **31** | **32** |
| Forward R; 1/2 Turn R | Back L; 1/2 Turn R | Forward R | Forward L |

Repeat entire dance. This is a one-wall dance.

Ghostbusters

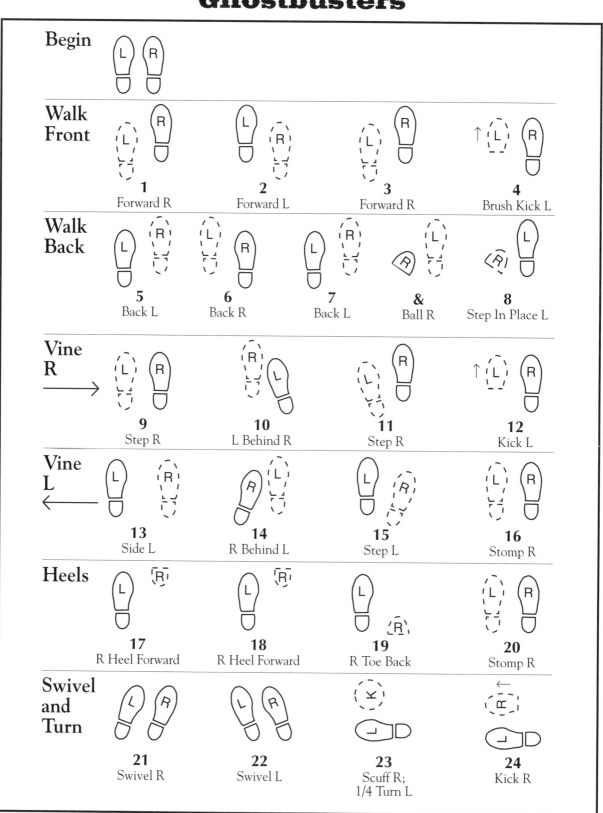

Begin			
Walk Front	**1** Forward R	**2** Forward L	**3** Forward R	**4** Brush Kick L
Walk Back	**5** Back L	**6** Back R	**7** Back L	**&** Ball R	**8** Step In Place L
Vine R	**9** Step R	**10** L Behind R	**11** Step R	**12** Kick L
Vine L	**13** Side L	**14** R Behind L	**15** Step L	**16** Stomp R
Heels	**17** R Heel Forward	**18** R Heel Forward	**19** R Toe Back	**20** Stomp R
Swivel and Turn	**21** Swivel R	**22** Swivel L	**23** Scuff R; 1/4 Turn L	**24** Kick R

Shuffle

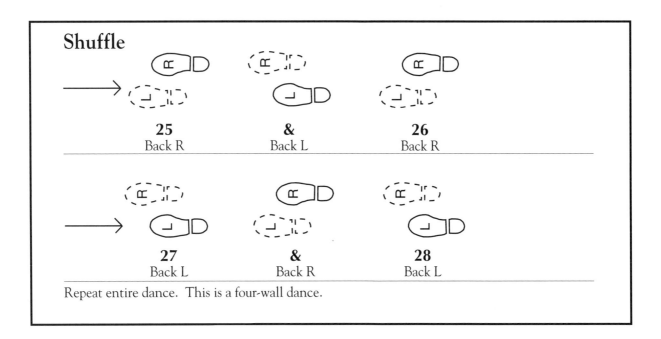

| **25** | **&** | **26** |
| Back R | Back L | Back R |

| **27** | **&** | **28** |
| Back L | Back R | Back L |

Repeat entire dance. This is a four-wall dance.

Honky Tonk Stomp

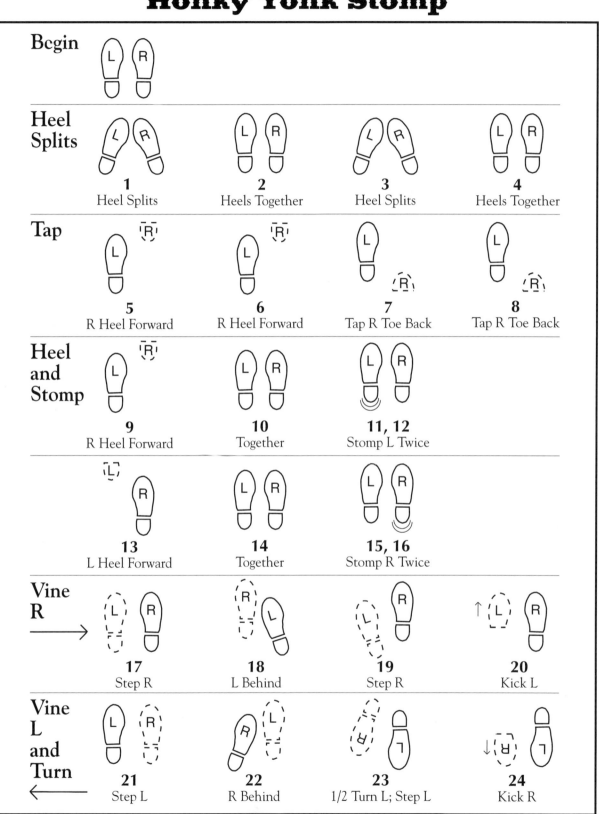

Begin			
Heel Splits	**1** Heel Splits	**2** Heels Together	**3** Heel Splits	**4** Heels Together
Tap	**5** R Heel Forward	**6** R Heel Forward	**7** Tap R Toe Back	**8** Tap R Toe Back
Heel and Stomp	**9** R Heel Forward	**10** Together	**11, 12** Stomp L Twice	
	13 L Heel Forward	**14** Together	**15, 16** Stomp R Twice	
Vine R →	**17** Step R	**18** L Behind	**19** Step R	**20** Kick L
Vine L and Turn ←	**21** Step L	**22** R Behind	**23** 1/2 Turn L; Step L	**24** Kick R

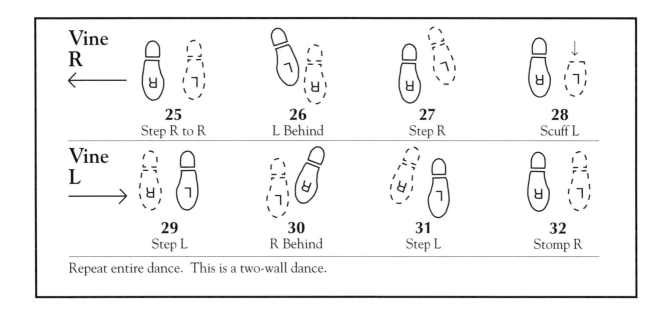

Vine R ←

25	**26**	**27**	**28**
Step R to R	L Behind	Step R	Scuff L

Vine L →

29	**30**	**31**	**32**
Step L	R Behind	Step L	Stomp R

Repeat entire dance. This is a two-wall dance.

Horseshoe Shuffle

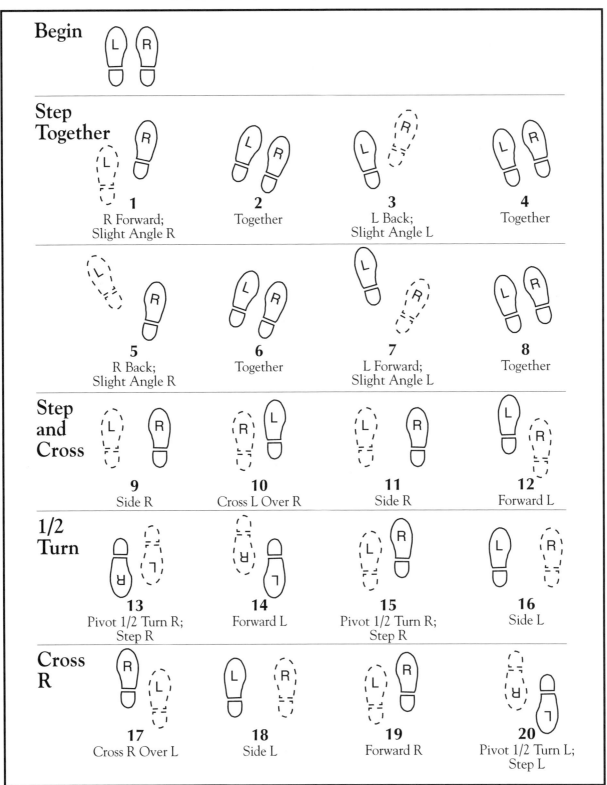

Begin

Step Together

1
R Forward;
Slight Angle R

2
Together

3
L Back;
Slight Angle L

4
Together

5
R Back;
Slight Angle R

6
Together

7
L Forward;
Slight Angle L

8
Together

Step and Cross

9
Side R

10
Cross L Over R

11
Side R

12
Forward L

1/2 Turn

13
Pivot 1/2 Turn R;
Step R

14
Forward L

15
Pivot 1/2 Turn R;
Step R

16
Side L

Cross R

17
Cross R Over L

18
Side L

19
Forward R

20
Pivot 1/2 Turn L;
Step L

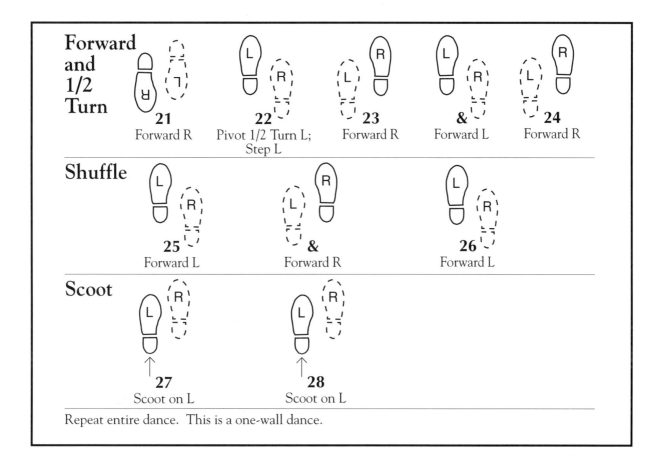

Forward and 1/2 Turn

21 Forward R

22 Pivot 1/2 Turn L; Step L

23 Forward R

& Forward L

24 Forward R

Shuffle

25 Forward L

& Forward R

26 Forward L

Scoot

27 Scoot on L

28 Scoot on L

Repeat entire dance. This is a one-wall dance.

Kokomo

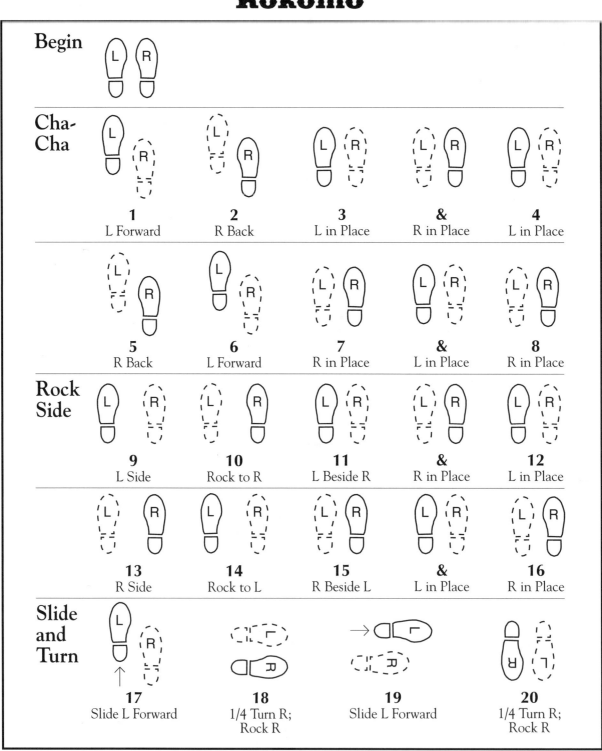

Begin				

Cha-Cha

1 L Forward	**2** R Back	**3** L in Place	**&** R in Place	**4** L in Place
5 R Back	**6** L Forward	**7** R in Place	**&** L in Place	**8** R in Place

Rock Side

9 L Side	**10** Rock to R	**11** L Beside R	**&** R in Place	**12** L in Place
13 R Side	**14** Rock to L	**15** R Beside L	**&** L in Place	**16** R in Place

Slide and Turn

17 Slide L Forward	**18** 1/4 Turn R; Rock R	**19** Slide L Forward	**20** 1/4 Turn R; Rock R

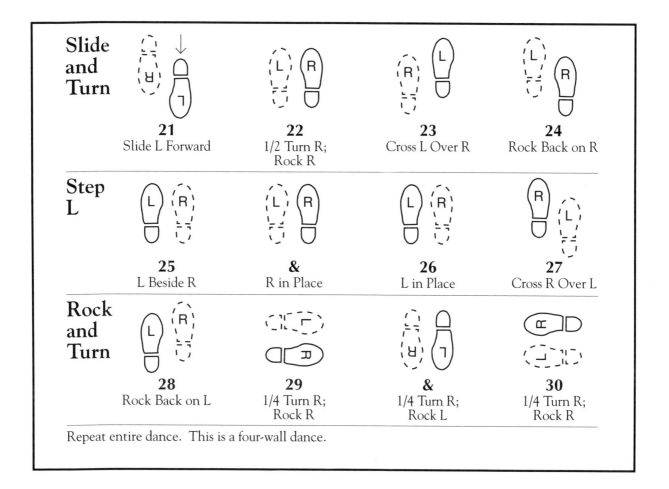

Slide and Turn

21
Slide L Forward

22
1/2 Turn R;
Rock R

23
Cross L Over R

24
Rock Back on R

Step L

25
L Beside R

&
R in Place

26
L in Place

27
Cross R Over L

Rock and Turn

28
Rock Back on L

29
1/4 Turn R;
Rock R

&
1/4 Turn R;
Rock L

30
1/4 Turn R;
Rock R

Repeat entire dance. This is a four-wall dance.

Louie

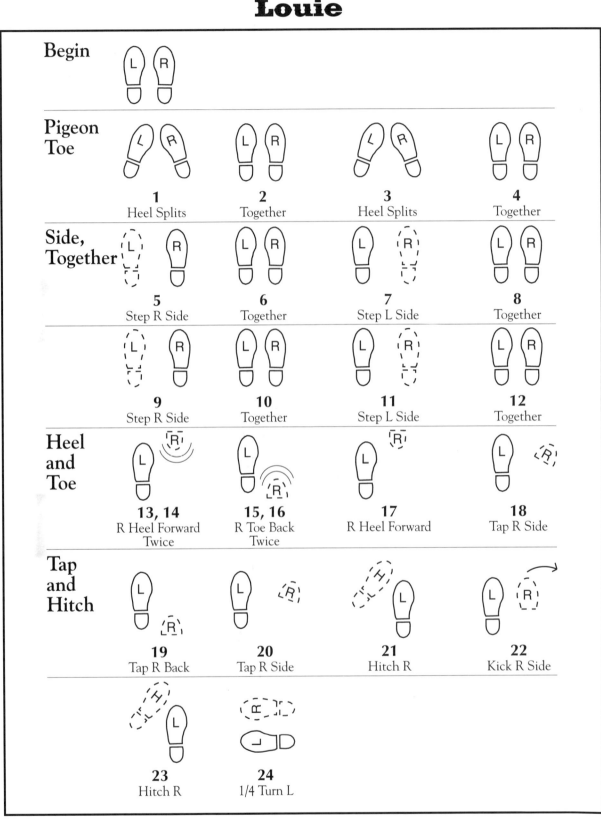

Begin

Pigeon Toe

1	2	3	4
Heel Splits	Together	Heel Splits	Together

Side, Together

5	6	7	8
Step R Side	Together	Step L Side	Together

9	10	11	12
Step R Side	Together	Step L Side	Together

Heel and Toe

13, 14	15, 16	17	18
R Heel Forward Twice	R Toe Back Twice	R Heel Forward	Tap R Side

Tap and Hitch

19	20	21	22
Tap R Back	Tap R Side	Hitch R	Kick R Side

23	24
Hitch R	1/4 Turn L

Vine R ↑

25	26	27	28
Step R Side	Cross L Behind R	R Side	Kick L

Vine L ↓

29	30	31	32
L Side	Cross R Behind L	L Side	Kick R

Back →

33	34	35	36
R Back	L Back	R Back	Kick L

Forward and Stomp

37	38
L Forward	Stomp R

Repeat entire dance. This is a four-wall dance.

Rockabilly Boogie

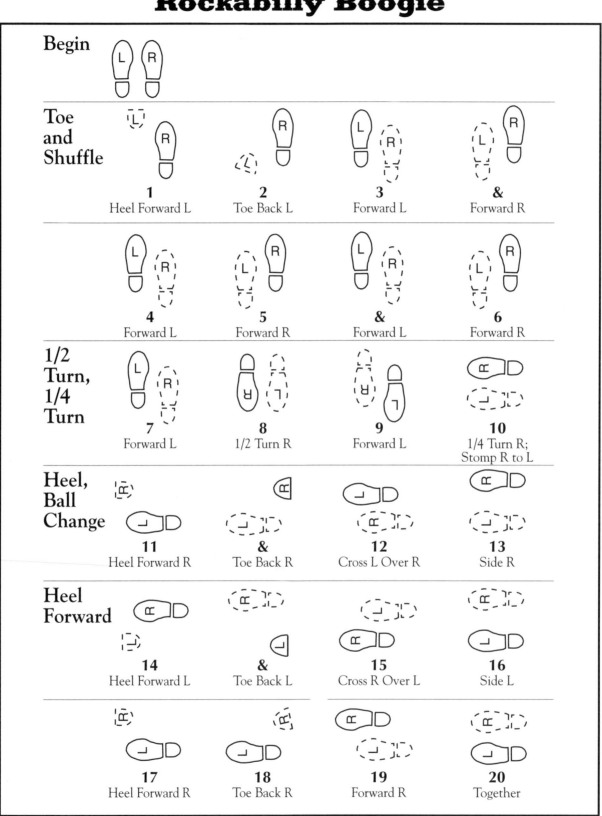

Begin			

Toe and Shuffle

1	2	3	&
Heel Forward L	Toe Back L	Forward L	Forward R

4	5	&	6
Forward L	Forward R	Forward L	Forward R

1/2 Turn, 1/4 Turn

7	8	9	10
Forward L	1/2 Turn R	Forward L	1/4 Turn R; Stomp R to L

Heel, Ball Change

11	&	12	13
Heel Forward R	Toe Back R	Cross L Over R	Side R

Heel Forward

14	&	15	16
Heel Forward L	Toe Back L	Cross R Over L	Side L

17	18	19	20
Heel Forward R	Toe Back R	Forward R	Together

Heels	**&** Lift Heels Up	**21** Place Heels Down	**&** Heels Up	**22** Heels Down
Back, Together	**23** Back R	**24** Together L	**&** Heels Up	**25** Heels Down
Heels	**&** Heels Up	**26** Heels Down	**27** L Step Diagonally Forward	**28** Hold
	29 R Step Diagonally Forward	**30** Hold	**31** L Step Diagonally Forward	**32** R Step Diagonally Forward
Forward and 1/4 Turn	**33** Forward L	**34** 1/4 Turn L; Tap R Back	**35** Brush R Forward	**36** Back Brush R Over L
Brush, Swivel	**37** Brush R Forward	**38** Together R	**39** Swivel Heels R	**40** Together
	41 Swivel Heels L	**42** Together		

Repeat entire dance. This is a two-wall dance.

Slappin' Leather

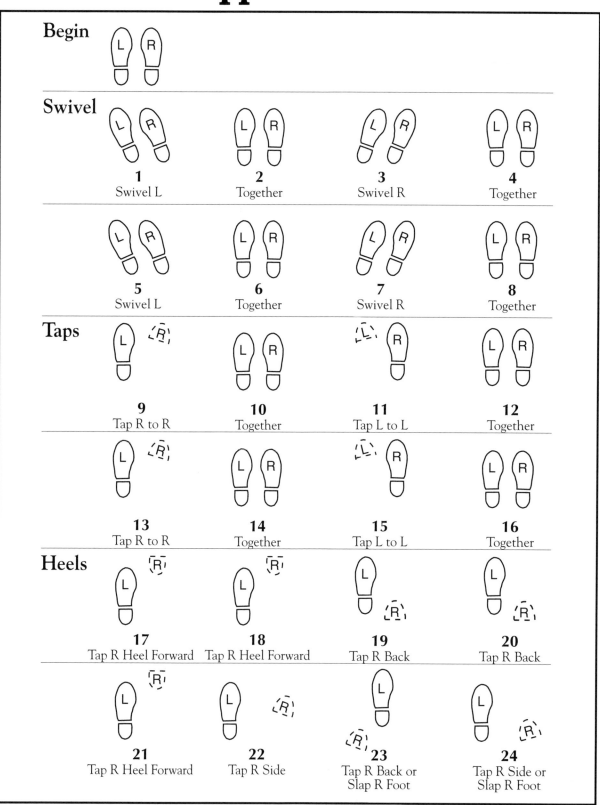

Begin			

Swivel

1
Swivel L

2
Together

3
Swivel R

4
Together

5
Swivel L

6
Together

7
Swivel R

8
Together

Taps

9
Tap R to R

10
Together

11
Tap L to L

12
Together

13
Tap R to R

14
Together

15
Tap L to L

16
Together

Heels

17
Tap R Heel Forward

18
Tap R Heel Forward

19
Tap R Back

20
Tap R Back

21
Tap R Heel Forward

22
Tap R Side

23
Tap R Back or
Slap R Foot

24
Tap R Side or
Slap R Foot

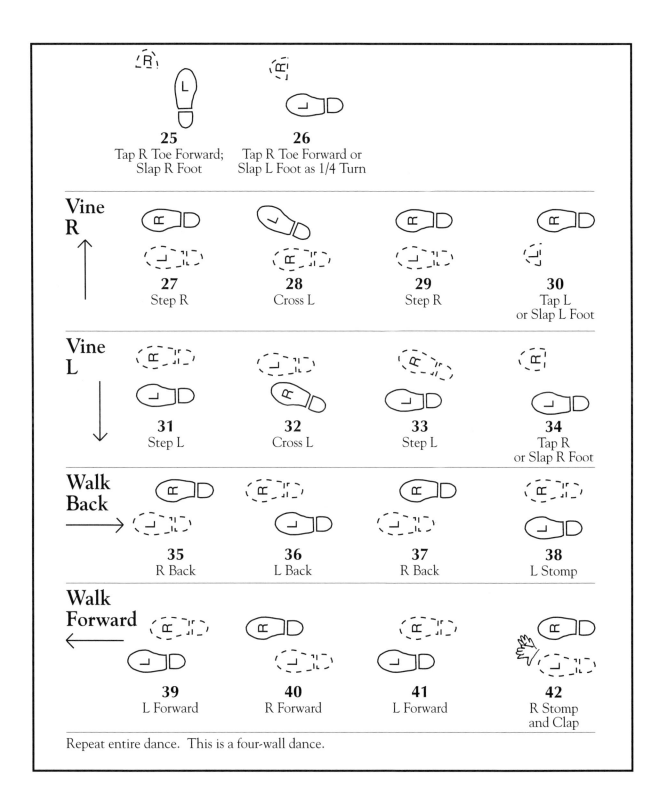

25
Tap R Toe Forward;
Slap R Foot

26
Tap R Toe Forward or
Slap L Foot as 1/4 Turn

Vine R

27
Step R

28
Cross L

29
Step R

30
Tap L
or Slap L Foot

Vine L

31
Step L

32
Cross L

33
Step L

34
Tap R
or Slap R Foot

Walk Back

35
R Back

36
L Back

37
R Back

38
L Stomp

Walk Forward

39
L Forward

40
R Forward

41
L Forward

42
R Stomp
and Clap

Repeat entire dance. This is a four-wall dance.

Thunderfoot

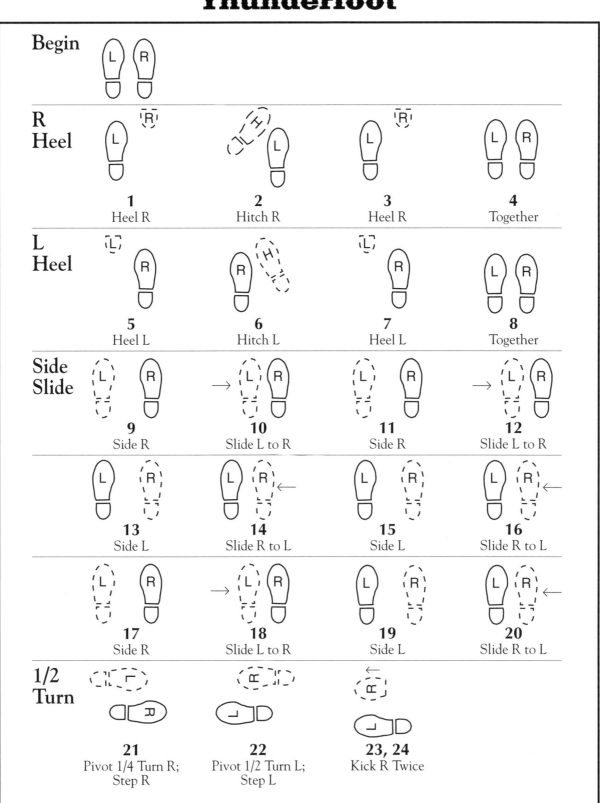

Begin			
R Heel			
1 Heel R	**2** Hitch R	**3** Heel R	**4** Together
L Heel			
5 Heel L	**6** Hitch L	**7** Heel L	**8** Together
Side Slide			
9 Side R	**10** Slide L to R	**11** Side R	**12** Slide L to R
13 Side L	**14** Slide R to L	**15** Side L	**16** Slide R to L
17 Side R	**18** Slide L to R	**19** Side L	**20** Slide R to L
1/2 Turn			
21 Pivot 1/4 Turn R; Step R	**22** Pivot 1/2 Turn L; Step L	**23, 24** Kick R Twice	

Back

25 Back R	**26** Back L	**27** Back R	**28** Back L

Forward Hitch

29 Forward R	**30** Hitch L	**31** Hitch R	**32** R Stomp

Heel Turn

33 Heel L	**34** Together	**35** Heel R	**36** Together

Repeat entire dance. This is a four-wall dance.

Tumbleweed

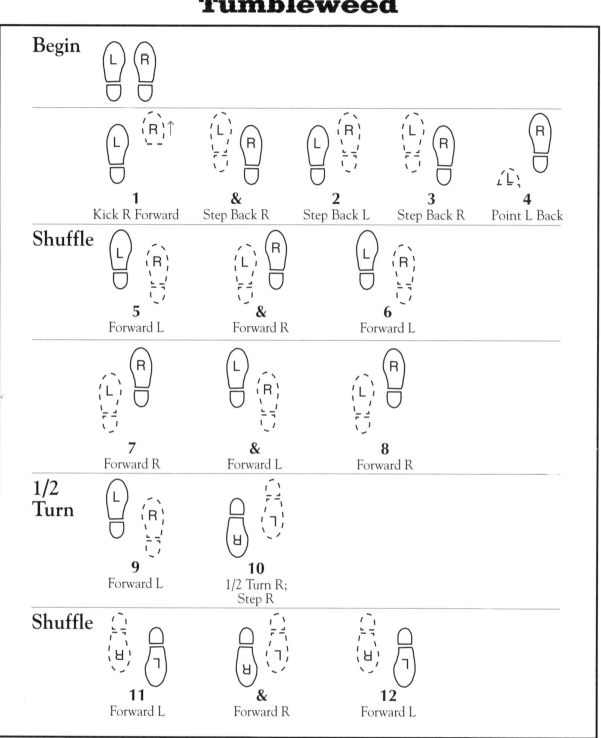

Begin

1	&	2	3	4
Kick R Forward	Step Back R	Step Back L	Step Back R	Point L Back

Shuffle

5	&	6
Forward L	Forward R	Forward L

7	&	8
Forward R	Forward L	Forward R

1/2 Turn

9	10
Forward L	1/2 Turn R; Step R

Shuffle

11	&	12
Forward L	Forward R	Forward L

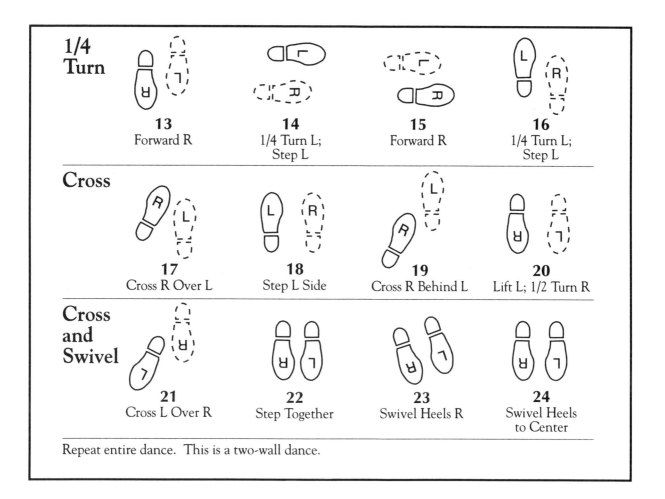

1/4 Turn

13
Forward R

14
1/4 Turn L;
Step L

15
Forward R

16
1/4 Turn L;
Step L

Cross

17
Cross R Over L

18
Step L Side

19
Cross R Behind L

20
Lift L; 1/2 Turn R

Cross and Swivel

21
Cross L Over R

22
Step Together

23
Swivel Heels R

24
Swivel Heels
to Center

Repeat entire dance. This is a two-wall dance.

Tush Push

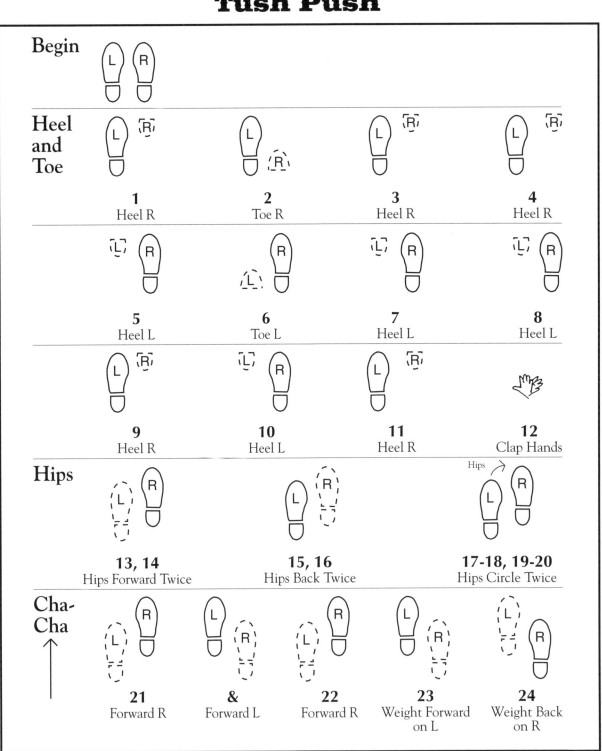

Begin

Heel and Toe

1	**2**	**3**	**4**
Heel R	Toe R	Heel R	Heel R

5	**6**	**7**	**8**
Heel L	Toe L	Heel L	Heel L

9	**10**	**11**	**12**
Heel R	Heel L	Heel R	Clap Hands

Hips

Hips

13, 14	**15, 16**	**17-18, 19-20**
Hips Forward Twice	Hips Back Twice	Hips Circle Twice

Cha-Cha

21	**&**	**22**	**23**	**24**
Forward R	Forward L	Forward R	Weight Forward on L	Weight Back on R

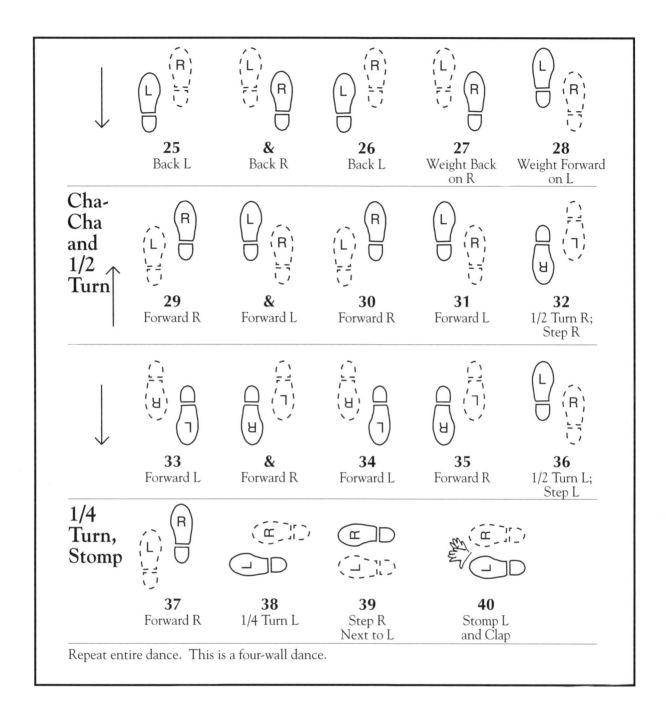

| **25** | **&** | **26** | **27** | **28** |
| Back L | Back R | Back L | Weight Back on R | Weight Forward on L |

Cha-Cha and 1/2 Turn

| **29** | **&** | **30** | **31** | **32** |
| Forward R | Forward L | Forward R | Forward L | 1/2 Turn R; Step R |

| **33** | **&** | **34** | **35** | **36** |
| Forward L | Forward R | Forward L | Forward R | 1/2 Turn L; Step L |

1/4 Turn, Stomp

| **37** | **38** | **39** | **40** |
| Forward R | 1/4 Turn L | Step R Next to L | Stomp L and Clap |

Repeat entire dance. This is a four-wall dance.

CHAPTER 5

When You Really Get Good...

Advanced Line Dances

If you've mastered the earlier dances and are ready for more of a challenge, these dances are for you! After you have mastered one dance, try dancing it to various types of music for variety. Pick up the speed (tempo) of music for a real challenge! Then try getting your brother or mother to do it with you! When you have some of these dances under your belt, read on to chapter 7, "Developing Style and Technique," where you will find some tricks on turning and some pointers on style. This is where real enjoyment comes in. After the left side of your brain conquers the dance (from considerable practice), the right side of your brain will help you begin to feel the mood of the music and to respond aesthetically. Enjoy!

Achy Breaky

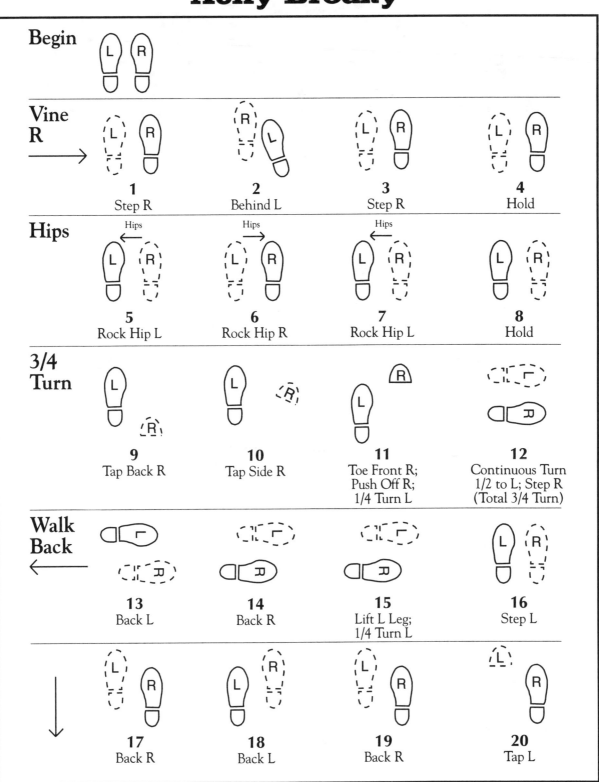

Begin			
Vine R →	**1** Step R	**2** Behind L	**3** Step R	**4** Hold
Hips	**5** Rock Hip L	**6** Rock Hip R	**7** Rock Hip L	**8** Hold
3/4 Turn	**9** Tap Back R	**10** Tap Side R	**11** Toe Front R; Push Off R; 1/4 Turn L	**12** Continuous Turn 1/2 to L; Step R (Total 3/4 Turn)
Walk Back ←	**13** Back L	**14** Back R	**15** Lift L Leg; 1/4 Turn L	**16** Step L
↓	**17** Back R	**18** Back L	**19** Back R	**20** Tap L

Hips

21	**22**	**23**	**24**
Rock Hip L	Rock Hip R	Rock Hip L	Hold

Step, Stomp

25	**26**	**27**	**28**
1/4 Turn R; Step R	Stomp L; Lift L	1/2 Turn L; Step L	Stomp R

Grapevine

29	**30**	**31**	**32**
Step R	Cross L Behind R	Step R	Stomp L; Clap Hands

Repeat entire dance. This is a four-wall dance.

Alley Cat

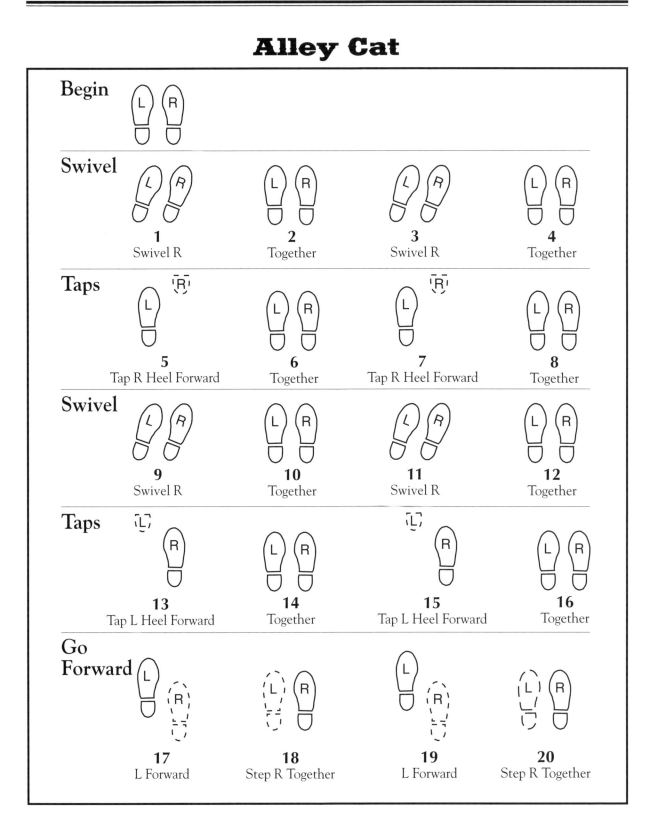

Begin

Swivel

1
Swivel R

2
Together

3
Swivel R

4
Together

Taps

5
Tap R Heel Forward

6
Together

7
Tap R Heel Forward

8
Together

Swivel

9
Swivel R

10
Together

11
Swivel R

12
Together

Taps

13
Tap L Heel Forward

14
Together

15
Tap L Heel Forward

16
Together

Go Forward

17
L Forward

18
Step R Together

19
L Forward

20
Step R Together

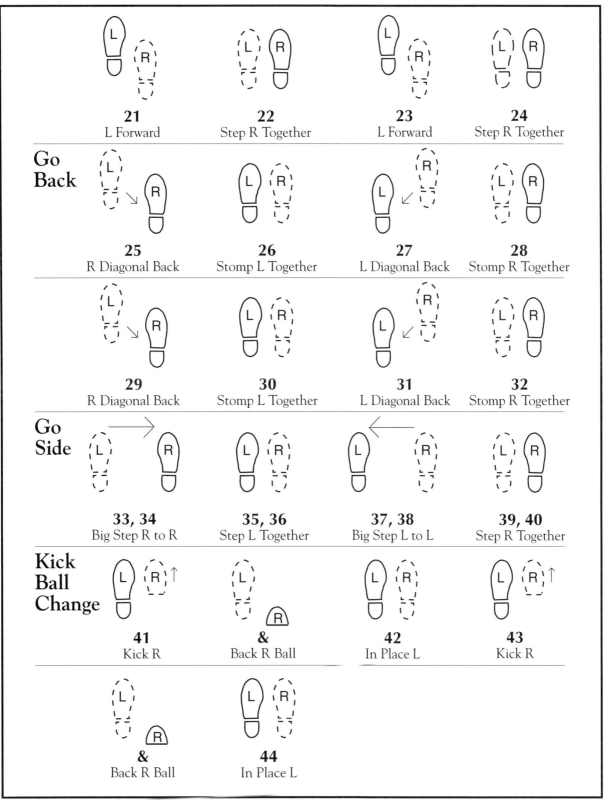

21
L Forward

22
Step R Together

23
L Forward

24
Step R Together

Go Back

25
R Diagonal Back

26
Stomp L Together

27
L Diagonal Back

28
Stomp R Together

29
R Diagonal Back

30
Stomp L Together

31
L Diagonal Back

32
Stomp R Together

Go Side

33, 34
Big Step R to R

35, 36
Step L Together

37, 38
Big Step L to L

39, 40
Step R Together

Kick Ball Change

41
Kick R

&
Back R Ball

42
In Place L

43
Kick R

&
Back R Ball

44
In Place L

(continued)

Alley Cat (*continued*)

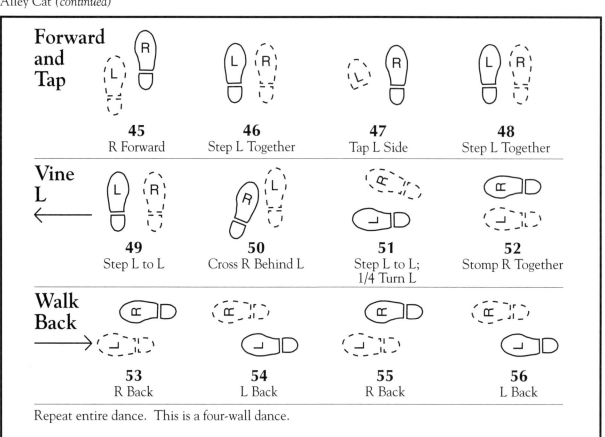

Forward and Tap

45 R Forward
46 Step L Together
47 Tap L Side
48 Step L Together

Vine L ←

49 Step L to L
50 Cross R Behind L
51 Step L to L; 1/4 Turn L
52 Stomp R Together

Walk Back →

53 R Back
54 L Back
55 R Back
56 L Back

Repeat entire dance. This is a four-wall dance.

Boot Scoot Boogie II

(Also known as "Boise Boot Scoot")

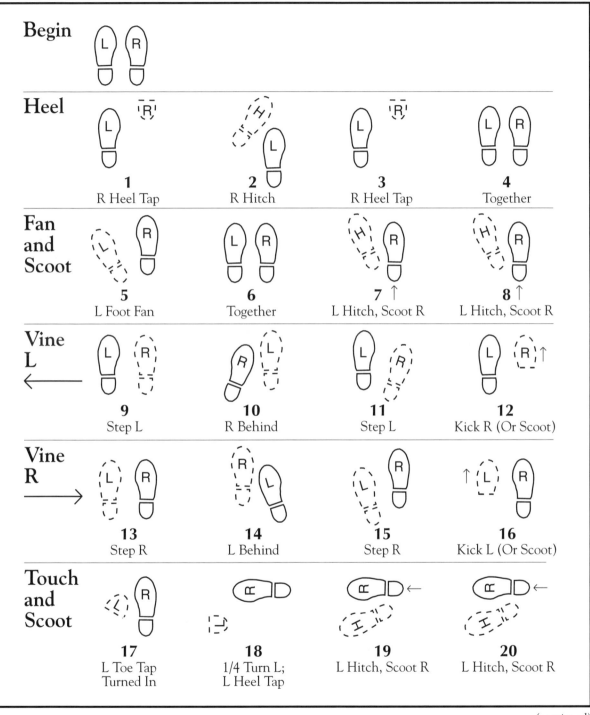

Begin

Heel

1	2	3	4
R Heel Tap	R Hitch	R Heel Tap	Together

Fan and Scoot

5	6	7 ↑	8 ↑
L Foot Fan	Together	L Hitch, Scoot R	L Hitch, Scoot R

Vine L ←

9	10	11	12
Step L	R Behind	Step L	Kick R (Or Scoot)

Vine R →

13	14	15	16
Step R	L Behind	Step R	Kick L (Or Scoot)

Touch and Scoot

17	18	19	20
L Toe Tap Turned In	1/4 Turn L; L Heel Tap	L Hitch, Scoot R	L Hitch, Scoot R

(continued)

Boot Scoot Boogie II *(continued)*

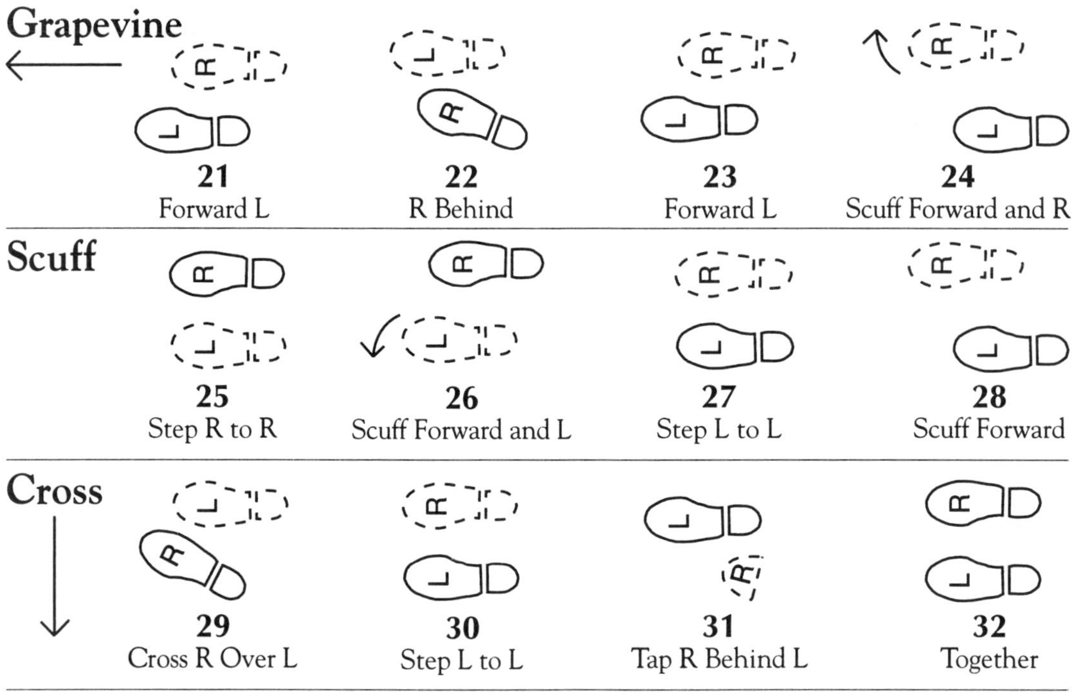

Grapevine

←——

21
Forward L

22
R Behind

23
Forward L

24
Scuff Forward and R

Scuff

25
Step R to R

26
Scuff Forward and L

27
Step L to L

28
Scuff Forward

Cross

29
Cross R Over L

30
Step L to L

31
Tap R Behind L

32
Together

Repeat entire dance. This is a four-wall dance.

Hip Hop

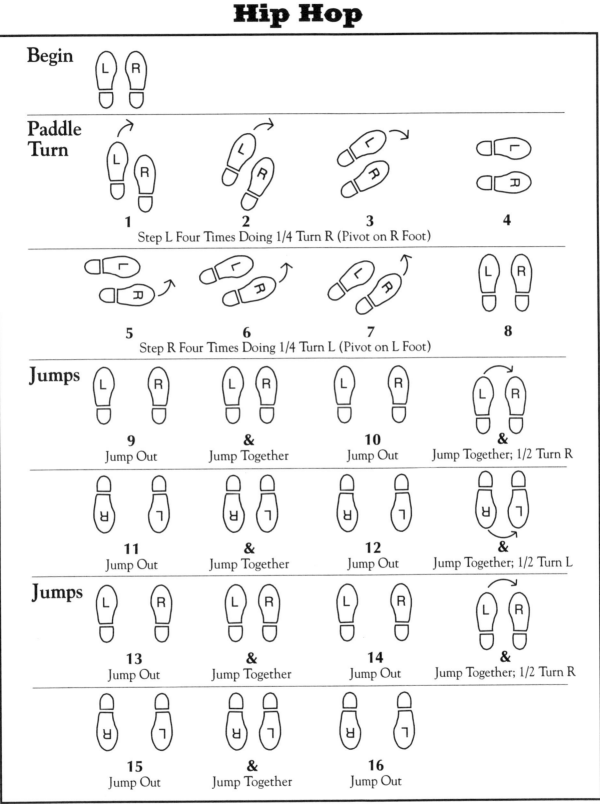

Begin

Paddle Turn

1   **2**   **3**   **4**

Step L Four Times Doing 1/4 Turn R (Pivot on R Foot)

5   **6**   **7**   **8**

Step R Four Times Doing 1/4 Turn L (Pivot on L Foot)

Jumps

| **9** | **&** | **10** | **&** |
| Jump Out | Jump Together | Jump Out | Jump Together; 1/2 Turn R |

| **11** | **&** | **12** | **&** |
| Jump Out | Jump Together | Jump Out | Jump Together; 1/2 Turn L |

Jumps

| **13** | **&** | **14** | **&** |
| Jump Out | Jump Together | Jump Out | Jump Together; 1/2 Turn R |

| **15** | **&** | **16** | |
| Jump Out | Jump Together | Jump Out | |

(continued)

Hip Hop *(continued)*

Paddle Turn

17 **18** **19** **20**

Step R Four Times Doing 1/4 Turn L (Pivot on L Foot)

Funky Kick

21 **&** **22** **&**
Kick L Back L Back R Forward L

23 **&** **24**
Scuff R 1/4 Turn L Stomp R

25-40
Repeat funky kick four more times; end facing front.

Vaudeville Step

41 **42** **&** **43**
Side L Cross R Side L Side R
Behind L

44 **&** **45**
Cross L Behind R Side R Together

46 **&** **47** **48**
Cross R Behind L Side L Forward R Side L

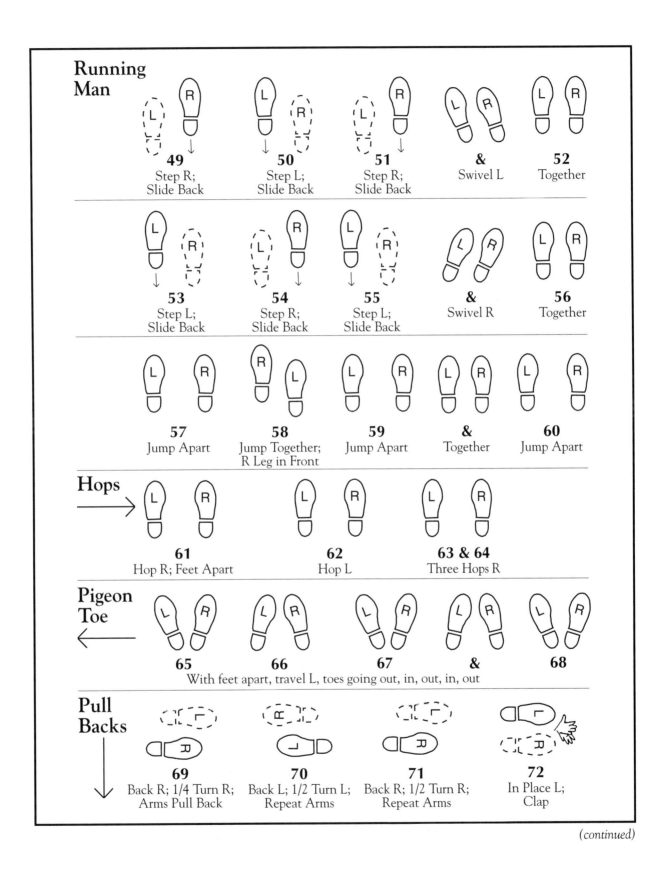

Running Man

49	50	51	&	52
Step R; Slide Back	Step L; Slide Back	Step R; Slide Back	Swivel L	Together

53	54	55	&	56
Step L; Slide Back	Step R; Slide Back	Step L; Slide Back	Swivel R	Together

57	58	59	&	60
Jump Apart	Jump Together; R Leg in Front	Jump Apart	Together	Jump Apart

Hops

61	62	63 & 64
Hop R; Feet Apart	Hop L	Three Hops R

Pigeon Toe

65	66	67	&	68

With feet apart, travel L, toes going out, in, out, in, out

Pull Backs

69	70	71	72
Back R; 1/4 Turn R; Arms Pull Back	Back L; 1/2 Turn L; Repeat Arms	Back R; 1/2 Turn R; Repeat Arms	In Place L; Clap

(continued)

Hip Hop (*continued*)

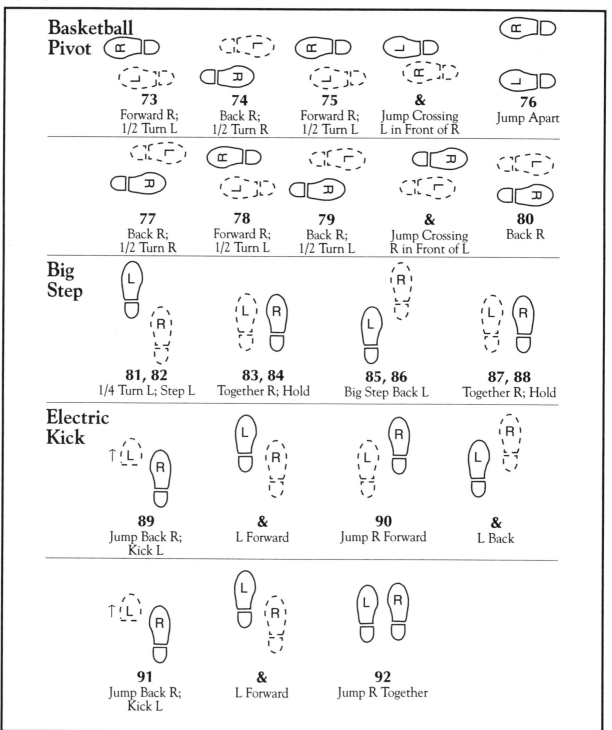

Basketball Pivot

73	74	75	&	76
Forward R; 1/2 Turn L	Back R; 1/2 Turn R	Forward R; 1/2 Turn L	Jump Crossing L in Front of R	Jump Apart

77	78	79	&	80
Back R; 1/2 Turn R	Forward R; 1/2 Turn L	Back R; 1/2 Turn L	Jump Crossing R in Front of L	Back R

Big Step

81, 82	83, 84	85, 86	87, 88
1/4 Turn L; Step L	Together R; Hold	Big Step Back L	Together R; Hold

Electric Kick

89	&	90	&
Jump Back R; Kick L	L Forward	Jump R Forward	L Back

91	&	92
Jump Back R; Kick L	L Forward	Jump R Together

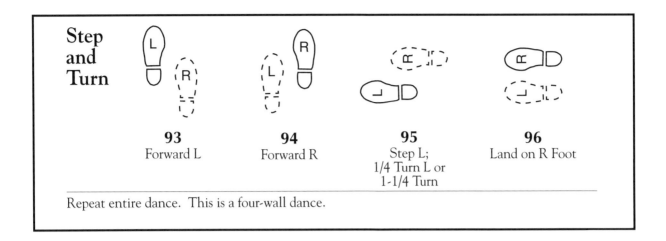

Step and Turn

| **93**
Forward L | **94**
Forward R | **95**
Step L;
1/4 Turn L or
1-1/4 Turn | **96**
Land on R Foot |

Repeat entire dance. This is a four-wall dance.

LeDoux Shuffle

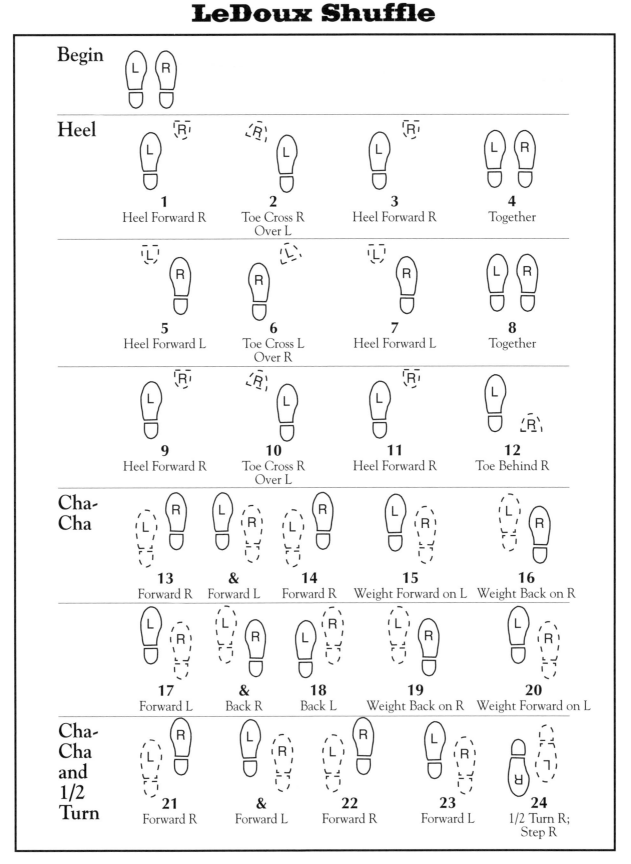

Begin

Heel

1 Heel Forward R	**2** Toe Cross R Over L	**3** Heel Forward R	**4** Together
5 Heel Forward L	**6** Toe Cross L Over R	**7** Heel Forward L	**8** Together
9 Heel Forward R	**10** Toe Cross R Over L	**11** Heel Forward R	**12** Toe Behind R

Cha-Cha

13 Forward R	**&** Forward L	**14** Forward R	**15** Weight Forward on L	**16** Weight Back on R
17 Forward L	**&** Back R	**18** Back L	**19** Weight Back on R	**20** Weight Forward on L

Cha-Cha and 1/2 Turn

21 Forward R	**&** Forward L	**22** Forward R	**23** Forward L	**24** 1/2 Turn R; Step R

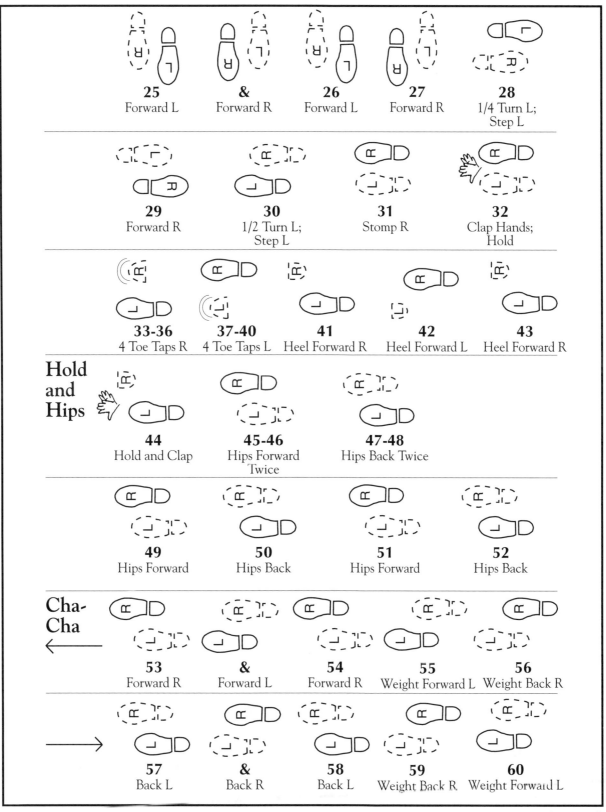

25 Forward L   **&** Forward R   **26** Forward L   **27** Forward R   **28** 1/4 Turn L; Step L

29 Forward R   **30** 1/2 Turn L; Step L   **31** Stomp R   **32** Clap Hands; Hold

33-36 4 Toe Taps R   **37-40** 4 Toe Taps L   **41** Heel Forward R   **42** Heel Forward L   **43** Heel Forward R

Hold and Hips

44 Hold and Clap   **45-46** Hips Forward Twice   **47-48** Hips Back Twice

49 Hips Forward   **50** Hips Back   **51** Hips Forward   **52** Hips Back

Cha-Cha

53 Forward R   **&** Forward L   **54** Forward R   **55** Weight Forward L   **56** Weight Back R

57 Back L   **&** Back R   **58** Back L   **59** Weight Back R   **60** Weight Forward L

(continued)

LeDoux Shuffle *(continued)*

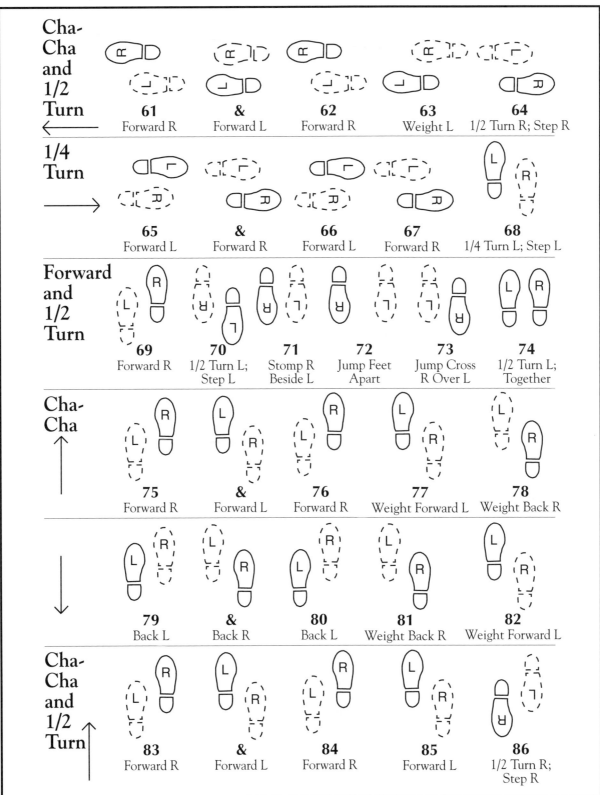

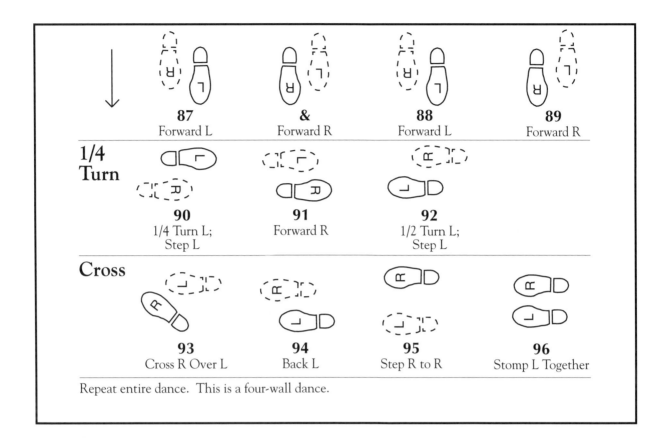

| **87** | **&** | **88** | **89** |
| Forward L | Forward R | Forward L | Forward R |

1/4 Turn

| **90** | **91** | **92** |
| 1/4 Turn L; Step L | Forward R | 1/2 Turn L; Step L |

Cross

| **93** | **94** | **95** | **96** |
| Cross R Over L | Back L | Step R to R | Stomp L Together |

Repeat entire dance. This is a four-wall dance.

Romeo

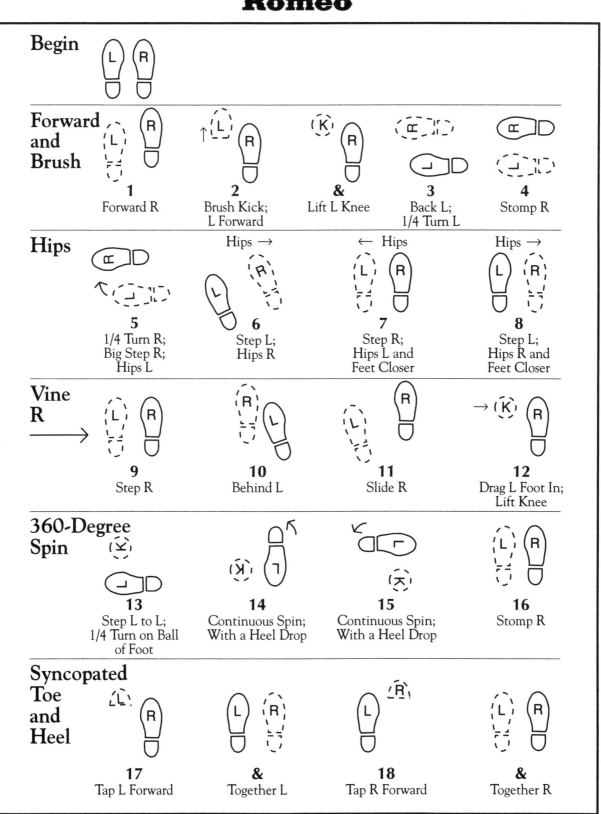

Begin

L R

Forward and Brush

1	2	&	3	4
Forward R	Brush Kick; L Forward	Lift L Knee	Back L; 1/4 Turn L	Stomp R

Hips

Hips →   ← Hips   Hips →

5	6	7	8
1/4 Turn R; Big Step R; Hips L	Step L; Hips R	Step R; Hips L and Feet Closer	Step L; Hips R and Feet Closer

Vine R →

9	10	11	12
Step R	Behind L	Slide R	Drag L Foot In; Lift Knee

360-Degree Spin

13	14	15	16
Step L to L; 1/4 Turn on Ball of Foot	Continuous Spin; With a Heel Drop	Continuous Spin; With a Heel Drop	Stomp R

Syncopated Toe and Heel

17	&	18	&
Tap L Forward	Together L	Tap R Forward	Together R

19
Tap L Behind R

&
Together L

20
Tap R Behind L

&
Together R

21
Tap L Side;
Toe In

&
Together L

22
Tap R Side;
Toe In

&
1/4 Turn L;
Together R

23
Tap L Heel

&
Step L

24
Tap R Toe Back

Hips

25
Weight on Ball
of R Forward; Hips R

26
Weight L;
Hips L

27
Weight on Ball
of R Back; Hips R

28
Weight L;
Hips L

Hips

Hips

Hips

Hips

29
Step R Ball Side;
Roll Hips to R

30
Step L Ball Side;
Roll Hips to L

31
Step R Ball Side;
Hips to R

32
Drop R Heel;
Weight L;
Hips L

Repeat entire dance. This is a four-wall dance.

Walkin' Wazi

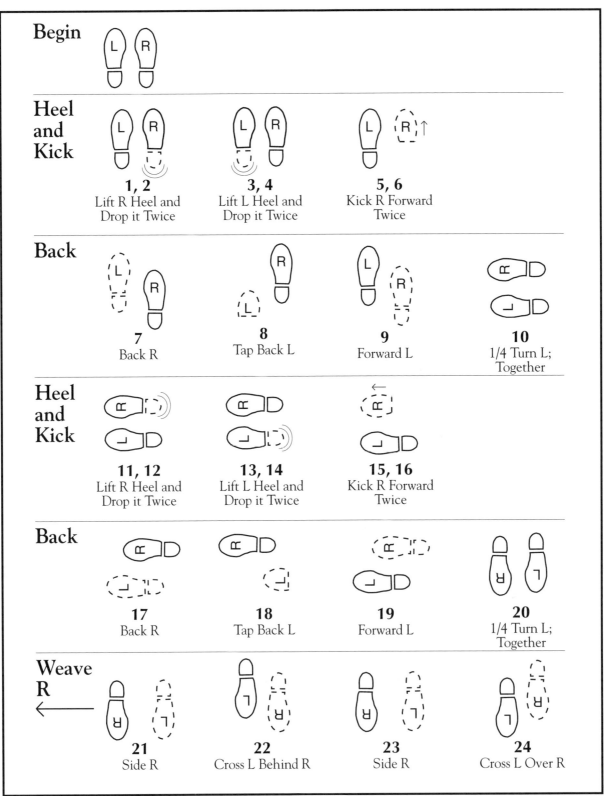

Begin

Heel and Kick

1, 2
Lift R Heel and Drop it Twice

3, 4
Lift L Heel and Drop it Twice

5, 6
Kick R Forward Twice

Back

7
Back R

8
Tap Back L

9
Forward L

10
1/4 Turn L; Together

Heel and Kick

11, 12
Lift R Heel and Drop it Twice

13, 14
Lift L Heel and Drop it Twice

15, 16
Kick R Forward Twice

Back

17
Back R

18
Tap Back L

19
Forward L

20
1/4 Turn L; Together

Weave R

21
Side R

22
Cross L Behind R

23
Side R

24
Cross L Over R

25	26	27	28
Side R	Cross L Behind R	Side R	Cross L Over R

1/4 Turn and Rock

29	30	31	32
1/4 Turn L; Hitch R	Step R	Shift Weight Back L	Shift Weight Forward R

1/2 Turns

33	34	35	36
Step L	1/2 Turn R; Step R	Step L	1/2 Turn R; Step R

37	38	39	40
Step L	1/2 Turn R; Step R	Step L	1/4 Turn L; Feet Together

Repeat entire dance. This is a two-wall dance.

CHAPTER 6

Share the Fun With Others!

Couples Pattern Dances, Mixers, and Icebreakers

Now that you have mastered the line dances and are feeling confident (I said confident, not cocky!), it is time to try something new. This chapter presents several line dances that you can do with a partner. It also includes mixers and icebreakers that you can do in a group, without requiring a partner. They're perfect for livening up a party. These dances will be great fun for everyone!

Couples Pattern Dances

Couples pattern dancing is line dancing with a partner. In this type of dancing couples perform the same patterned foot movement holding on to each other in selected arm positions. They travel in the line of dance repeating the sequence until the music ends. Sounds fun, huh?

The arm positions for the following dances are the sweetheart position (also known as the side-by-side position; see Figure 6.1), the modified sweetheart position (also known as the dancing skaters position; see Figure 6.2), the double-handhold position (see Figure 6.3), and the country-western closed position (see Figure 6.4). In the sweetheart position, the couple faces the line of dance joining hands. The lady is on the guy's right side. The partners hold right hands slightly in front of the lady's right shoulder and left hands slightly in front of the lady's left shoulder. The modified sweetheart position is similar to the sweetheart position except that the woman is slightly in front of the man's right hip and the right hands rest on the woman's right hip. The partners join left hands in front of the man at chest level. In the double-handhold position the couple faces each other while holding hands, with the woman's hands on top and her fingers in the man's palms. The couple also faces each other in the country-western closed position, but the man holds the woman's right hand in his left at shoulder height. His right hand is on her left shoulder, while the woman's left hand rests on the man's upper right arm.

Note that in all dances in this chapter, men and women do the same footwork, unless specified otherwise. Well, that's about it. You already know the basic steps and terminology, so let's do it!

Figure 6.1 *Sweetheart position.*

Figure 6.2 *Modified sweetheart position.*

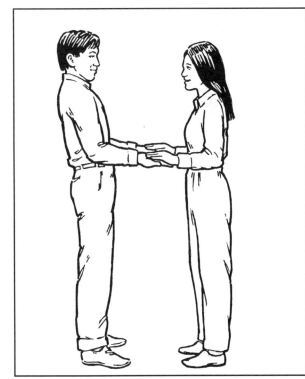

Figure 6.3 *Double-handhold position.*

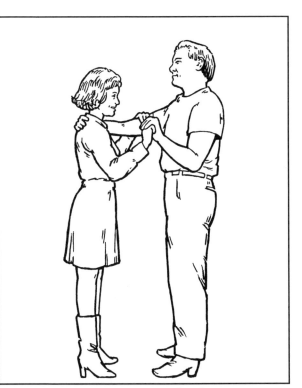

Figure 6.4 *Country-western closed position.*

Breezy

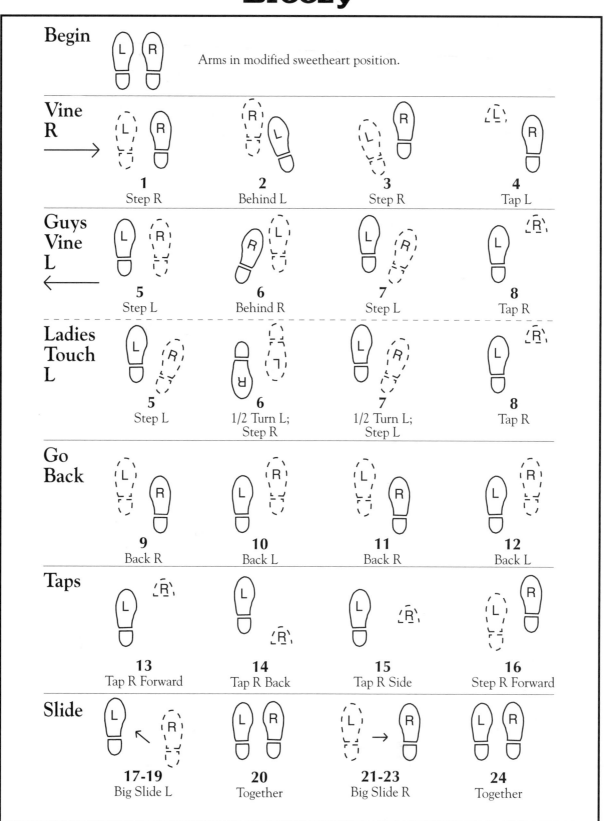

Begin

Arms in modified sweetheart position.

Vine R →

1	2	3	4
Step R	Behind L	Step R	Tap L

Guys Vine L ←

5	6	7	8
Step L	Behind R	Step L	Tap R

Ladies Touch L

5	6	7	8
Step L	1/2 Turn L; Step R	1/2 Turn L; Step L	Tap R

Go Back

9	10	11	12
Back R	Back L	Back R	Back L

Taps

13	14	15	16
Tap R Forward	Tap R Back	Tap R Side	Step R Forward

Slide

17-19	20	21-23	24
Big Slide L	Together	Big Slide R	Together

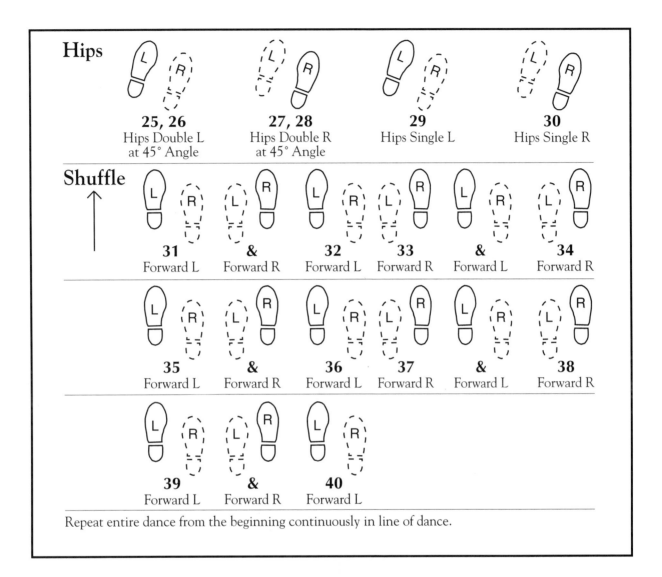

Hips

25, 26
Hips Double L
at 45° Angle

27, 28
Hips Double R
at 45° Angle

29
Hips Single L

30
Hips Single R

Shuffle

31
Forward L

&
Forward R

32
Forward L

33
Forward R

&
Forward L

34
Forward R

35
Forward L

&
Forward R

36
Forward L

37
Forward R

&
Forward L

38
Forward R

39
Forward L

&
Forward R

40
Forward L

Repeat entire dance from the beginning continuously in line of dance.

Cotton Eyed Joe

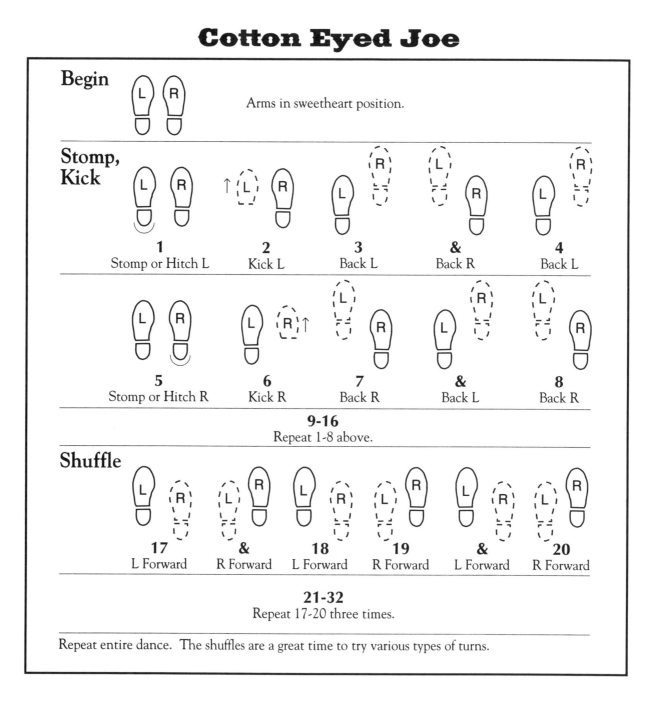

Begin

Arms in sweetheart position.

Stomp, Kick

1	2	3	&	4
Stomp or Hitch L	Kick L	Back L	Back R	Back L

5	6	7	&	8
Stomp or Hitch R	Kick R	Back R	Back L	Back R

9-16
Repeat 1-8 above.

Shuffle

17	&	18	19	&	20
L Forward	R Forward	L Forward	R Forward	L Forward	R Forward

21-32
Repeat 17-20 three times.

Repeat entire dance. The shuffles are a great time to try various types of turns.

Longhorn Special

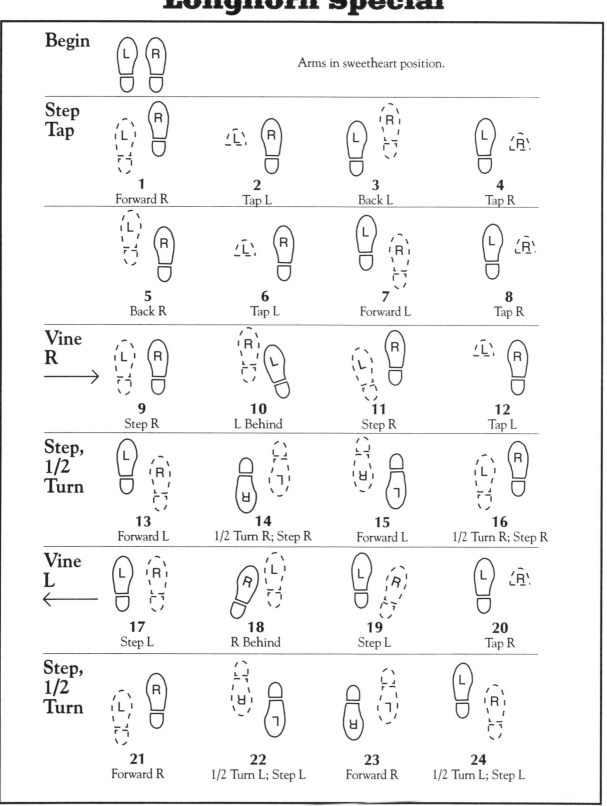

Begin — Arms in sweetheart position.

Step Tap
1 Forward R
2 Tap L
3 Back L
4 Tap R
5 Back R
6 Tap L
7 Forward L
8 Tap R

Vine R →
9 Step R
10 L Behind
11 Step R
12 Tap L

Step, 1/2 Turn
13 Forward L
14 1/2 Turn R; Step R
15 Forward L
16 1/2 Turn R; Step R

Vine L ←
17 Step L
18 R Behind
19 Step L
20 Tap R

Step, 1/2 Turn
21 Forward R
22 1/2 Turn L; Step L
23 Forward R
24 1/2 Turn L; Step L

(continued)

Longhorn Special (*continued*)

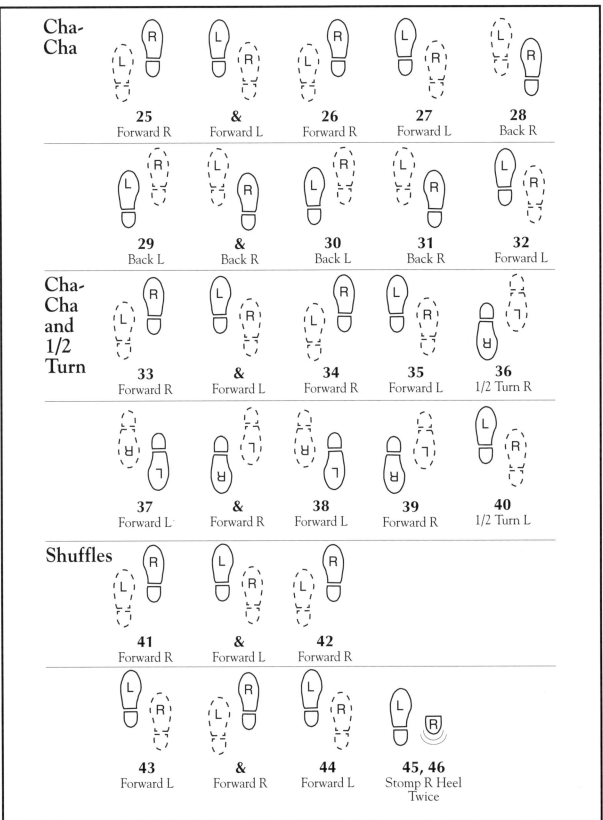

Cha-Cha	**25** Forward R	**&** Forward L	**26** Forward R	**27** Forward L	**28** Back R
	29 Back L	**&** Back R	**30** Back L	**31** Back R	**32** Forward L
Cha-Cha and 1/2 Turn	**33** Forward R	**&** Forward L	**34** Forward R	**35** Forward L	**36** 1/2 Turn R
	37 Forward L	**&** Forward R	**38** Forward L	**39** Forward R	**40** 1/2 Turn L
Shuffles	**41** Forward R	**&** Forward L	**42** Forward R		
	43 Forward L	**&** Forward R	**44** Forward L	**45, 46** Stomp R Heel Twice	

47-54
Repeat shuffles 41-44 twice.

55-56
Repeat stomps 45-46.

Repeat entire dance in line of dance.

Ten-Step

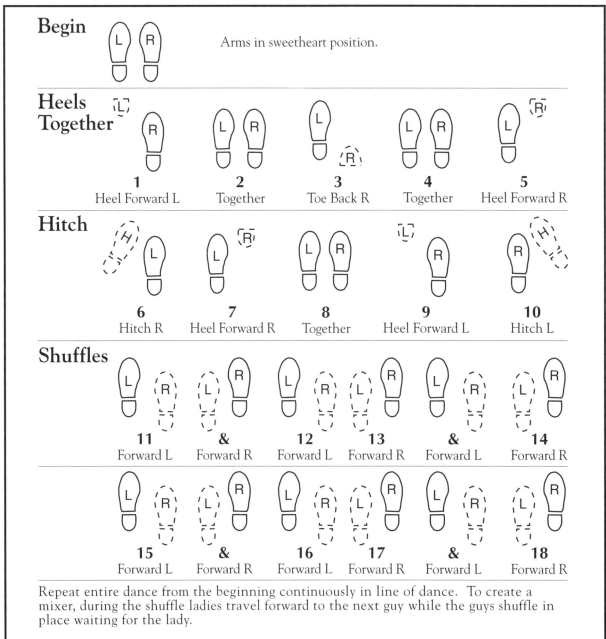

Begin   Arms in sweetheart position.

Heels Together

1	2	3	4	5
Heel Forward L	Together	Toe Back R	Together	Heel Forward R

Hitch

6	7	8	9	10
Hitch R	Heel Forward R	Together	Heel Forward L	Hitch L

Shuffles

11	&	12	13	&	14
Forward L	Forward R	Forward L	Forward R	Forward L	Forward R

15	&	16	17	&	18
Forward L	Forward R	Forward L	Forward R	Forward L	Forward R

Repeat entire dance from the beginning continuously in line of dance. To create a mixer, during the shuffle ladies travel forward to the next guy while the guys shuffle in place waiting for the lady.

Traveling Cha-Cha

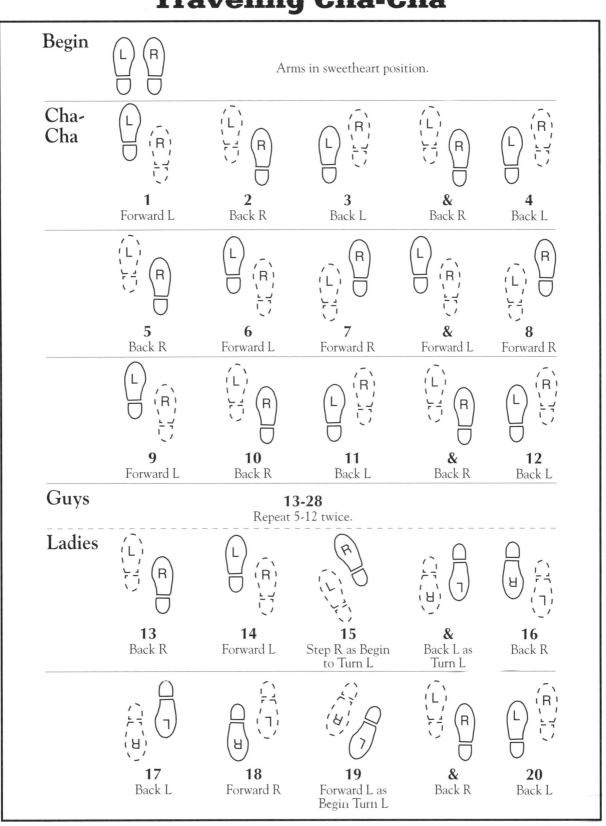

Begin

Arms in sweetheart position.

Cha-Cha

| **1** | **2** | **3** | **&** | **4** |
| Forward L | Back R | Back L | Back R | Back L |

| **5** | **6** | **7** | **&** | **8** |
| Back R | Forward L | Forward R | Forward L | Forward R |

| **9** | **10** | **11** | **&** | **12** |
| Forward L | Back R | Back L | Back R | Back L |

Guys

13-28
Repeat 5-12 twice.

Ladies

| **13** | **14** | **15** | **&** | **16** |
| Back R | Forward L | Step R as Begin to Turn L | Back L as Turn L | Back R |

| **17** | **18** | **19** | **&** | **20** |
| Back L | Forward R | Forward L as Begin Turn L | Back R | Back L |

(continued)

Traveling Cha-Cha (*continued*)

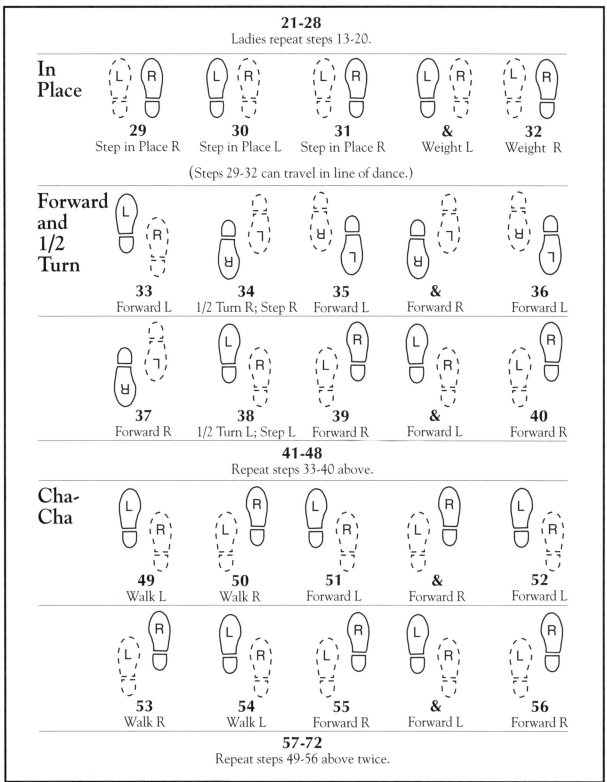

21-28
Ladies repeat steps 13-20.

In Place

29	30	31	&	32
Step in Place R	Step in Place L	Step in Place R	Weight L	Weight R

(Steps 29-32 can travel in line of dance.)

Forward and 1/2 Turn

33	34	35	&	36
Forward L	1/2 Turn R; Step R	Forward L	Forward R	Forward L

37	38	39	&	40
Forward R	1/2 Turn L; Step L	Forward R	Forward L	Forward R

41-48
Repeat steps 33-40 above.

Cha-Cha

49	50	51	&	52
Walk L	Walk R	Forward L	Forward R	Forward L

53	54	55	&	56
Walk R	Walk L	Forward R	Forward L	Forward R

57-72
Repeat steps 49-56 above twice.

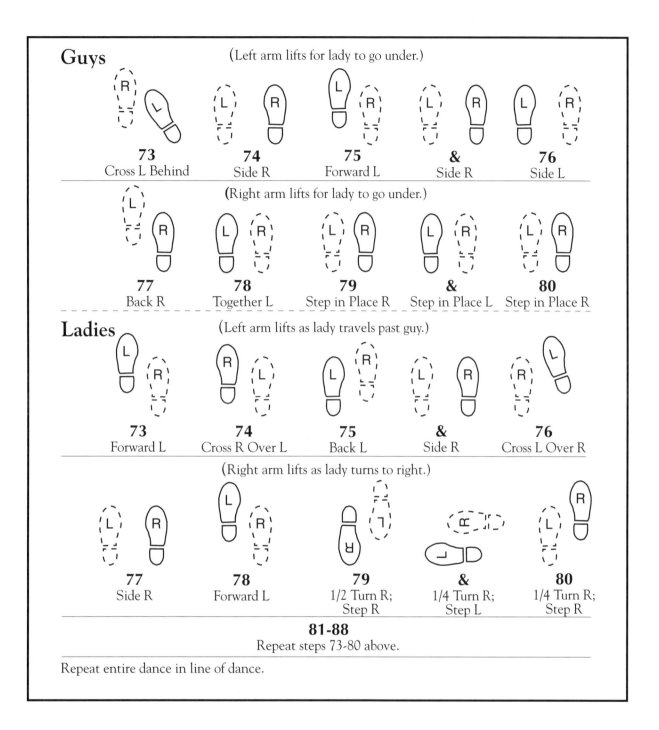

Guys (Left arm lifts for lady to go under.)

73	**74**	**75**	**&**	**76**
Cross L Behind	Side R	Forward L	Side R	Side L

(Right arm lifts for lady to go under.)

77	**78**	**79**	**&**	**80**
Back R	Together L	Step in Place R	Step in Place L	Step in Place R

Ladies (Left arm lifts as lady travels past guy.)

73	**74**	**75**	**&**	**76**
Forward L	Cross R Over L	Back L	Side R	Cross L Over R

(Right arm lifts as lady turns to right.)

77	**78**	**79**	**&**	**80**
Side R	Forward L	1/2 Turn R; Step R	1/4 Turn R; Step L	1/4 Turn R; Step R

81-88
Repeat steps 73-80 above.

Repeat entire dance in line of dance.

Mixers and Icebreakers

Here's the scenario. You have a room filled with people and you want to turn the place into laughter and excitement. What do you do? A mixer or icebreaker, of course! They "break the ice" by being simple, fun, and not requiring a partner. They are great ideas for parties and social events.

Mixers are dances in which new partners are acquired after the sequence of steps. You can perform these dances without changing partners, but that is why they are so much fun!

Icebreakers do not require a partner at all. The Bunny Hop and Conga are performed in a "conga" line (single file). The participant places his or her hands on the waist of the person in front and performs the designated footwork. The Hokey Pokey and the Bird Dance are danced either in one big circle with everyone facing inside the circle or scattered throughout the room. The Stroll, also known as the Soul Train Line, is performed in two lines. Always a fun dancing game is good ol' Musical Chairs. So go ahead, try it; I guarantee a good time for all.

Barn Dance

Partners begin facing each other in the double-handhold position and move in the line of dance. Guys are on the inside of the dance floor, ladies on the outside of the dance floor.

Note: Arm position can also be in a country-western closed position.

Guys	Step L to L	Together	Step L to L	Tap R
Ladies	Step R to R	Together	Step R to R	Tap L
	1	**2**	**3**	**4**
Guys	Step R to R	Together	Step R to R	Tap L
Ladies	Step L to L	Together	Step L to L	Tap R
	5	**6**	**7**	**8**
Guys	Step L to L	Together	Step L to L	Tap R
Ladies		Three-Step Turn to Right (R L R)		Tap L
	9	**10**	**11**	**12**
Guys	Step R to R	Together	Step R to R	Tap L
Ladies		Three-Step Turn to Left (L R L)		Tap R
	13	**14**	**15**	**16**
Guys	Face LOD; Step L	Hop on L	Step R	Hop on R
Ladies	Face LOD; Step R	Hop on R	Step L	Hop on L
	17	**18**	**19**	**20**
Guys	Step L	Hop on L	Step R	Hop on R
Ladies	Step R	Hop on R	Step L	Hop on L
	21	**22**	**23**	**24**

(Grapevine Facing LOD)

Guys	Step L to L	Cross R Behind L	Step L to L	Tap R
Ladies	Step R to R	Cross L Behind R	Step R to R	Tap L
	25	**26**	**27**	**28**

(Grapevine or Turn Toward Circle to Another Partner)

Guys		Four-Step Turn Right (R L R L)		
Ladies		Four-Step Turn Left (L R L R)		
	29	**30**	**31**	**32**

Ladies will take a new partner coming from the left.

Repeat entire dance continuously in line of dance.

Bunny Hop

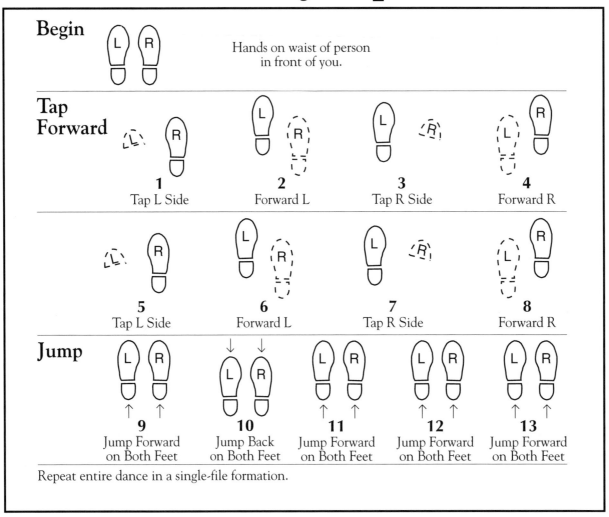

Begin

Hands on waist of person
in front of you.

Tap Forward

1 Tap L Side

2 Forward L

3 Tap R Side

4 Forward R

5 Tap L Side

6 Forward L

7 Tap R Side

8 Forward R

Jump

9 Jump Forward on Both Feet

10 Jump Back on Both Feet

11 Jump Forward on Both Feet

12 Jump Forward on Both Feet

13 Jump Forward on Both Feet

Repeat entire dance in a single-file formation.

Conga

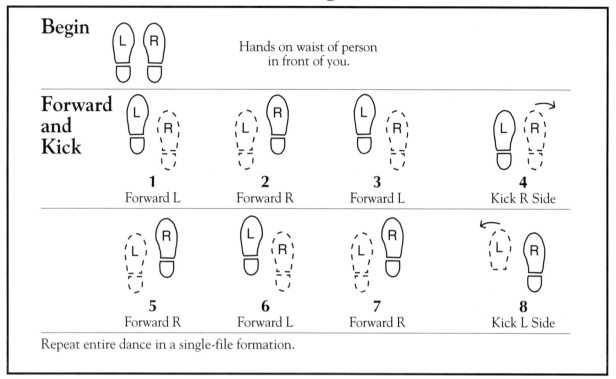

Begin Hands on waist of person in front of you.

Forward and Kick

1 Forward L **2** Forward R **3** Forward L **4** Kick R Side

5 Forward R **6** Forward L **7** Forward R **8** Kick L Side

Repeat entire dance in a single-file formation.

Hokey Pokey

Everyone forms a circle facing inward and performs the movements to the words of the song. Try to imitate all the words of the song as the lyrics change.

"You Put Your Right Foot In"

Place your right foot toward the inside of the circle.

"You Put Your Right Foot Out"

Place your right foot behind you to the outside of the circle.

"You Put Your Right Foot in and You Shake It All About"

Place your right foot toward the inside of the circle and shake it.

"You Do the Hokey Pokey"

Point the index finger on your right hand toward the ceiling and wiggle your hips.

"And You Turn Yourself About"

Shake your hands overhead as you turn in a circle.

"That's What It's All About"

Clap your hands four times.

Repeat, using the body part given in each verse of the song.

Bird Dance

Everyone forms a circle or is scattered throughout the room.

Counts 1-4

Make a beak with both hands and imitate a bird singing.

Counts 5-8

Make wings by putting your hands under your armpits and flapping your wings.

Counts 9-12

Do the twist as far down as you can go.

Counts 13-16

Come up doing the twist and clapping your hands four times.

Rest of Chorus

Grab a partner, lock arms, and do-si-do.

Repeat throughout the song.

Stroll

Everyone forms two straight lines, with the men in one line and the women in another, facing each other. The first couple joins together and "strolls" or freestyles down the center of the lines. When they get to the end, they take their places at the end of the two straight lines and wait until their turn comes up again. Sometimes the two lines will be uneven in number and thus the couple may acquire new partners! While the couples stroll or dance freestyle down the center, people in the lines on the sides perform a grapevine to the right and left continuously in unison. Everyone gets a chance to show off!

Musical Chairs

The traditional and ever-so-popular musical chairs is a great way to get people moving! Set a number of chairs around in a circle one fewer in quantity than the number of people participating. Then play whatever music your heart desires as everyone begins to walk in a clockwise circle around the chairs. When you stop the music, the participants run to the nearest chair and sit down *fast*. The one participant who does not get a chair is eliminated. You then take out another chair until all the chairs are gone except one. The person left at the end of the game who claims the last chair is the winner.

Developing Style and Technique

All right! We are now ready to shine! Here are some pointers to give you that extra special flair on the dance floor.

Technique

Although you will find some differences in techniques throughout the country, most line dancing today is performed with a country-western technique. The most common approach is to carry your weight over the ball of the foot. As you walk forward, your steps swing in front of your hips with your toe skimming the floor. Backward steps also swing from the hips, with the toe skimming the floor and the heel reaching back to gain full extension on each step. The knees flex slightly, neither straight nor bent. Straight legs take away from the smoothness and grace in dancing. The ideal country-western dancer is smooth, so try not to bounce. Let your upper torso glide while your lower body does all the work. Relax your shoulders. In contrast, a funky dancer picks up the feet and utilizes the upper body, letting the rib cage, shoulders, and head move as much as possible while freestyling with the arms. Buy yourself a video camera and watch yourself dance. It is an excellent training aid.

Style

Style is the essence of creativity. It is the personal expression given to dance through your body carriage and feeling. It allows freedom for individual interpretation and improvisation. Next time you practice dancing, turn the music on and permit your body to move freely to the beat you hear. Do whatever comes naturally; nothing is right or wrong.

One way to help your body feel the music is through body awareness exercises called *isolation exercises*. By practicing moving different parts of your body, you become more conscious of how the body moves. For example, let's focus on the hip movements used in dances such as the Tush Push. Stand center, facing in one direction with your feet apart. Bend your knees and push your hips to the right and then to the left. Repeat slowly and continuously, then increase the speed of the isolated hip movements. Next, move your hips forward and back. After increasing the speed, try some hip rolls to the right and then to the left.

If you want to try the line dances with a funky flair, try to isolate the rib cage the same way you isolated your hips. Move the rib cage only, side to side (this is going to feel very strange!), then front to back. Moving the rib cage when you are dancing enhances the funky look.

And what about your head? Are you holding it stiff as a board while you dance? Try grapevining to the right and to the left and relaxing the head slightly by nodding it up and down while you move. Feel the tension relax in the neck as if you were constantly saying "yes!" Continue doing the grapevine, only this time concentrate on your shoulders. Move them any way you want—up and down, forward or back, or shake them side to side.

Now that you have tried isolating these different parts of the body, practice performing various line dances and be attentive to what the different parts of the body do as you dance. Your awareness and coordination will increase with every part of your body you can integrate into your steps.

Variations

One way to spice up your dancing is with variations, such as fancy turns and spins. For example, whenever a grapevine is called in a line dance, substitute a turn. Here are some techniques that will help your turns.

As I mentioned in chapter 1, good posture is essential in dance and is a tremendous source of control, especially when turning. If your body falls out of alignment even slightly, the turning "force" will throw you off balance. Control your arms, don't let them just hang. When turning to the left, concentrate on the rotation of the shoulders turning left. Spot by focusing your eyes on an object after you have turned. Country-western style dancing does not have sharp spotting techniques like you would see in ballet.

Timing in turns is developed through consistent practice. The timing will feel different when you perform two rotations as compared to three or four turns on one leg. Speed will be greater as you increase the number of turns. You will need to find your own timing. Try practicing turning at different tempos and speeds.

Some additional special tips include these:

1. Strengthening the abdominal muscles through proper sit-up exercises will help you control your posture when executing turns.

2. Strengthening your calf muscles will help you hold the position on the ball of the foot needed to do multiple turns. Practice lifting your heels off the floor and returning to the ground 15 times. It is a good idea to stretch those calf muscles, too!

3. When you are executing multiple turns, visualize yourself performing 10 more turns than you were planning on doing. Visualization is beneficial in helping you expand the amount of turns you can get your body to do.

Attitude

This brings us to the mental rehearsal, which is just as important as the physical practice. One of the most difficult obstacles for dancers, especially for beginners, is to forget their self-consciousness and "let go." As a novice, or even an advanced student, you may feel some negative emotions—for example, nervous tension, anxiety, or maybe even low self-esteem—getting in your way. How can you get rid of these psychological barriers?

It takes training—a form of mental training that you must develop just as you develop a muscle through physical training. Visualize yourself dancing. Believe in yourself and mentally see yourself accomplishing your goals. Visualization works best when you are relaxed. Breathing into the abdomen is one of the most valuable techniques for focusing, calming, and energizing yourself. Have confidence. Confidence is the quality that refuses to stay defeated, a kind of stubborn cheerfulness. Confidence is learned, and nothing can stop you from attaining it.

The biggest anxiety producer is yourself. Everyone seems to feel pressures and self-doubts, even good dancers. Good dancers just know how to handle them better. To better channel your emotional anxiety, become aware of your body and mind by tuning into your feelings and emotions. Then relax both mind and body by letting go and breathing deeply and easily. Remain focused on your dancing in a positive way and always visualize yourself making the dance moves you desire. This mental rehearsal makes developing self-confidence a habit and your reactions become automatic. Reminisce on a positive moment when everything seemed to flow. Remember the harmony of your body and mind and how it felt. This is the state you want to reach . . . when you commit every aspect of yourself to the movement. Whatever it takes for you, mental rehearsal is a good idea if you want to perform well and enjoy a meaningful inner experience. So practice mentally as well as physically.

For Teachers Only

You do not have to be a great dancer to be a great teacher. In fact, the trained dancer has an advantage over someone who is a "natural dancer" because the trained dancer can relate better to skill development and student needs. One thing is for certain: To be a good educator, you must have a keen desire to help others.

Use this checklist if you are interested in becoming a line dance instructor. Put a check by the areas in which you feel qualified:

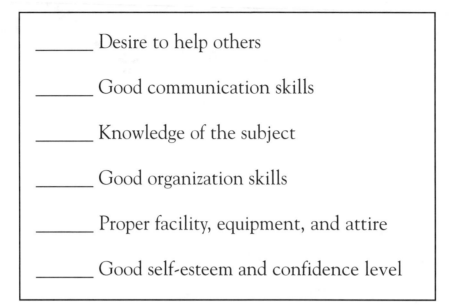

_____ Desire to help others

_____ Good communication skills

_____ Knowledge of the subject

_____ Good organization skills

_____ Proper facility, equipment, and attire

_____ Good self-esteem and confidence level

If you have checked off every quality and are not currently instructing, try it. Teaching dance can be hard work, but there is no better reward than helping others. If you checked off only a few of the qualities, there is always time to develop the others if you truly wish to teach.

Let's talk about how to put together the ingredients of a good line dance class.

Facility

First, of course, you need a facility. Before you get too excited and build a brand new building to teach your line dancing classes, consider establishing a following of students. Teaching part-time in an already established organization such as a nightclub, dance studio, or school gymnasium is a great way to get started. Nightclub owners are always looking for a way to bring people in, so classes offered before the evening crowd arrives may prove to be your best bet. You can work on a commission or salary. You may have to deal with people smoking and using alcohol in a nightclub, however, so if that is not your desire, you may prefer employment by a local community center, YMCA, YWCA, recreation department, Boys or Girls Club, or continuing education program.

Be aware of floor friction when choosing a surface for dancing. A wood floor is the best type of floor to dance on, so a gym floor would be a better surface to use than a cafeteria floor, which is often concrete. A dance studio is a great place for line dance instruction because people come there strictly to dance, it has mirrors, and it is a more professional environment. Be careful of a rubber floor called marlee, which is popular in the dance studios that offer ballet, however. Rubber flooring of any type can be a real hindrance to line dancing instruction. A disadvantage of instructing at a private dance studio is that you will be competing against other types of dance instruction for studio space in the prime time slots. Many health clubs or aerobic schools offer line dance aerobics. Because the specialized floors in these locations are made for tennis shoes rather than cowboy boots, you may feel comfortable teaching a line dance class in tennis shoes, but be aware you cannot slide much.

Of course any building large enough to accommodate the number of dancers you wish to teach at one time would work. Just avoid carpeted floor and rooms with beams (so you don't have to worry about bumping into them), and be sure the acoustics are clear. Echoes are very frustrating for participants trying to hear the beat. Proper ventilation and circulation are necessities. Be sure restrooms and drinking water are readily available. (Remember, soda pop and alcohol can dehydrate your students, making them feel tired.) If you live in a comfortable outdoor environment, like the desert, the Hawaiian islands, or the South, dancing outside is a marvelous experience. (Line dancing under a palm tree does wonders for the soul!)

Equipment

For equipment, of course, you will need an adequate sound system. If you are teaching at a dance club, dance studio, or health club, chances are the house system is good, which means one less investment for you. But if you travel to teach on special occasions or if you are in an unequipped gym or building, you will have to consider three different types of sound systems.

The least expensive sound system is a high-quality boom box consisting of a portable cassette deck, a compact disc player, or both. Having a dual cassette deck gives you the added advantage of being able to cue the next song while you are playing another, so there is no dead time in class. This is fine for a small group in an indoor area; it is also inexpensive and easy to cart around. The disadvantages to using a boom box as your music system are that it often does not provide enough volume for large groups, and you cannot attach a microphone to it.

The next higher grade of sound system is a more expensive self-contained unit that comes with a speed control cassette deck (which is extremely beneficial when instructing beginning students), microphone, amplifier, and speaker. A typical system includes an institutional case with a handle and is approximately 15 in. wide by 24 in. high with an average weight of 21 lbs. This kind of system is great for instructing medium-size groups because it is louder and clearer than a boom box, it has a microphone, and it is easy to transport. The disadvantages are that most systems of this type do not work with cordless microphones, and their loudness is limited. In addition, speakers on these systems face only one direction, hearing is limited, and the microphone may create interference if you stand in front of the speaker.

The best equipment is a professional sound system similar to that used by disc jockeys. This type of system should not be confused with a home sound system: A professional system is much more durable and can provide greater amplification without damaging the speakers. A complete system includes an amplifier; cassette deck, compact disc player, or both; mixing board; microphone; speakers; and a case. The most important benefits of using a professional system are the sound quality and volume. A good standard to use for instructing a large group in a building such as a gymnasium is 250 watts per speaker. This type of system gives you complete control over the volume of your voice in relationship to your music. Its higher quality microphone— either a wireless, lapel, or headset—and amplifier provide good clarity with no interference. You should be able to move your head while you are talking and walk anywhere in the building without any interference or fluctuation in the voice. The mixing board adjusts the volume of the microphone in relation to the music and can give you the freedom of playing music continuously from your compact disc player to your cassette deck—just like a disc jockey. The cassette deck with a speed control is a wonderful method of teaching. You can purchase speakers separately to accommodate the volume needed for your facility and the size of your group, but they must be compatible with your amplifier. A compact disc player that comes with a remote can be an advantage if you are helping students on the dance floor and you do not have time to run back to the sound system to change the music . . . just press the remote! All these units can be purchased individually to satisfy your needs, and most contain a 3-year warranty. The sound system can fit into a rack mountable case for easy storage and mobility. Of course, you will need a bigger budget for this type of investment. Ask a professional for assistance in matching your system to your needs.

Music

And now for the music. What music do you play? What if students do not like your music? Relax. Just like a disc jockey, you must play a variety. Watch how your students react to the songs. Be assertive, but do not stray away from the popular songs. Maybe you have heard a particular song over and over again, but your students haven't. Be open! Remember, you are serving your students.

If you still use phonograph albums, be prepared—they will be harder and harder to purchase in the future. Cassettes and compact discs are your best bet. Compact discs (CDs) have an advantage over cassettes not only because of their sound quality, but also because you do not have to waste time rewinding and fast-forwarding. Students waiting for an instructor to fiddle with equipment often lose motivation. If your only option is a cassette player, try recording each song you wish to play on a single cassette so you can just pick up the cassette and go.

You may want to prerecord your favorite music on cassette yourself so it plays continuously as you teach. Or you can contact an aerobic music service company. Be aware that a lot of the songs these companies provide are not by the original artists, but are remakes of the originals, or many are tunes that have not hit the top of the charts.

What music should you use? Well, first off, see Appendix B for a recommended music list that was put together based on a national survey. Or you can check the latest charts in your local record stores for a listing of the 10 top sellers. Your local disc jockey may be able to give you more advice. Being on top of the latest music is always an advantage in teaching; however, it can get expensive. Talk to the manager at your local record store and ask for an instructor's discount if you refer students' business to the store. Another idea is to have students bring in music they enjoy. Always review the music for bad lyrics and proper beats per minute before playing it in class. Try a few line dances to it. If your time is limited, join a mail-order music club, but be aware that these clubs may require contracts and their prices are sometimes higher than your local music store.

If you are self-employed you must obtain license to use the music you choose from the American Society of Composers, Authors and Publishers (ASCAP) and Broadcast Music, Inc. (BMI). You'll find information about these companies in the Resources. If you teach in a dance club, health club, or school, check with your facility manager to be sure the organization is licensed. Also, you may consider liability insurance.

Attire

Here's a small hint . . . your clothing should be clean and appropriate for the setting. Dress like a professional. Your personal attire creates an atmosphere and motivates your students. Because line dancing class is similar to a social event, dress in the proper social attire. Make sure your students feel comfortable in what they are wearing to help increase their confidence levels. If your line dancing class is funky, everything goes! For shoes, cowboy boots or a comfortable walking shoe are the best, but almost any type of shoe can do with the exception of shoes with rubber soles, shoes with heels, and sandals. (Just think of the liability problem you may have if someone's sandals fly off and hit someone else while you are teaching a kick!) Of course, socks and bare feet are not suitable. In health clubs, the main focus is physical fitness, so the appropriate attire for this environment is loose-fitting clothing or sweats with aerobic shoes. Students wearing tennis shoes should use caution when doing turns and pick up their feet to avoid ankle problems.

Class Format

Now that you're sounding good and looking good, let's talk about the class format. The most successful formula for teaching class is to offer a 6- to 8-week course that meets once a week for 1 to 2 hours. This length will neither discourage the beginners nor bore the more experienced students. When you begin your next session, do not be discouraged if students do not return; turnover is expected. There are many reasons why students may not want to continue, ranging from not having enough time to feeling that they have enough material to keep them happy for awhile. As you begin the new line dance session, offer two courses: one for beginners and one for intermediate level (people who are returning). At the end of this session offer another series of courses and add an advanced level. From here, after observing class enrollment, you will have to determine whether you should keep channeling students into the advanced level or create new classes, perhaps ones that combine the intermediate and advanced levels. As the advanced level continues, offer variety in the classes such as working on style, performing in groups, or preparing students for a dance competition.

Let's pretend this is your first day of class and you are encountering butterflies in your stomach. What is the very first thing you should do? *Relax and talk* to the students. *Be yourself*. Students love honesty. Then begin your lesson with a class format such as the following and adjust the time to fit your designated teaching time slot.

1. *Welcome the class.* Give them a general orientation on what to expect. This will help them prepare mentally and emotionally. Give the students a chance to get to know each other by having them meet someone new and shake hands or by telling you the name of their favorite song. Always encourage verbal sharing of ideas.

2. *Put on some popular music and GET MOVING.* A secret about teaching . . . keep your students active and they will have an enjoyable experience. If this is an advanced class, review some previously learned line dances. If this is a beginners class, have the students practice walking patterns and marching in place to music. You can actually teach some of the movements, especially those accompanied by fast music, by half counting (stepping on every other beat) while continuously repeating the terminology and keeping the students moving. If this is the second or third class, review any dances already learned.

3. *Present a new line dance and always start with a beginning dance.* Teach the new dance step-by-step and build on each progression. Keep repeating the name of the dance as you teach it. Teach the dance at a slow tempo and repeat, repeat, repeat! Teach the dance facing one wall, even if the dance is a two- or four-wall dance, until the students are proficient. If you do not have mirrors, demonstrate the dances with your back to the students. Then when you feel the students are ready, walk through the dance facing the different directions (or walls) before doing it to music. Only teach a few phrases at a time and repeat, making sure the majority have it before you continue on. Nothing is more frustrating for a student than to be taught too much at one time. A good exercise is to have students close their eyes as you call out the steps slowly. Another exercise is to have the students count the beats out loud as they practice to the beat of music. If you have a student with absolutely no rhythm, keep encouraging him or her to practice and perhaps offer half-hour private lessons before or after class at a reduced rate.

4. *Try the new dance to different songs and tempos.* This will keep the class interested and motivated. Let the students talk after they have learned a sequence. It gives them the opportunity to relax and release tension. Encouraging a social atmosphere is one of the objectives of dance.

5. *Schedule a break to discuss details, review the entire dance slowly, give pointers, and work on style.* Encourage dancers to drink water. Encourage questions. During this time you can show videotapes of TV shows or discuss retail outlets for music and attire and places to go dancing. Or bring in a guest teacher.

6. *Repeat complete dances again until the class is proficient (which means the majority have it).* Then review any previously learned dances one right after the other, making sure the majority have successfully completed each dance before going on to the next one. Always keep the music going! This will give the students a sense of accomplishment as well as inspire them to keep dancing.

7. *Allow 5 minutes at the end of class for questions or individual attention and "bonding."* This is a great time for teachers because it is when they get their best feedback and have a chance to get to know class participants personally. This will also keep your following class on time. Remember, people are working their schedules to fit you! So be on time! Be sure to tell the students a little bit about your next lesson so they have something to look forward to.

8. *Make notes of what you have taught and jot down ideas for the next class while fresh in your mind.* The best time to prepare for your next lesson is when everything is still on your mind.

If you are teaching an *aerobics* line dance class, your format will be different. You should be certified aerobically (see the Resources). The following format is based on a 40- to 60-minute class:

5-10 minutes   Get the body temperature up by doing walking patterns. If this is not your first class, review previously learned line dances.

3-5 minutes   Stretch the appropriate muscle groups, making sure the calves, hamstrings, and hip area are warmed up sufficiently.

20-30 minutes   Perform continuous line dance patterns facing one wall until the class is proficient enough to face other walls. It is important to keep the class moving. Implement marches in place as you "add on" the line dance movements in proper progression. The marches allow students to relax mentally and prepare for the next dance step. Add arm and upper body movements to expand the workout. Be sure to decrease the beats per minute during the last 5 minutes (cool-down).

10-15 minutes   If time permits, include conditioning for the abdominal muscles and upper torso area.

5 minutes   Cool-down with slow stretching movements.

Additional Suggestions

Be prompt, organized, and ready to take control. Most students attend class because of you, so having a regular substitute teacher is not a good idea if you want students to come back.

Be positive to create an emotionally safe and fun learning environment. Have a sense of humor and be friendly, enthusiastic, and personable. Remember, most of your students take the class for recreational reasons, not to become professional dancers.

Be firm, yet compassionate. Establish whatever rules are necessary to maintain control. Take responsibility for your authority, but be sensitive to the students' feelings.

Know your students. Learn their names and the types of music they enjoy. Be a good listener. A good teacher is a good learner. Make your students feel important. Be flexible. Adapt to your group. Your students will respect you if you keep up-to-date.

Use good eye contact. Do not favor individual students. Make corrections on a positive note—reinforcing what the student should do, rather than what the student should not do. Students should never be afraid of making a mistake.

Give clear directions. Keep your instructions light, not too technical. Try to cue before the movement. Call out the detailed steps first, then abbreviate the cues to the suggested words listed with each dance. Finally, call out the number of counts in the line dance. Ask your local microphone salesman the correct way to speak into your microphone to get the best effect. Soda pop and alcohol dehydrate you and hamper your speaking ability.

Adapt to your students' ages and their ability levels. If you are teaching young children and they are having difficulty learning the routine, simplify it with an easier variation. But be sure the students know that the dance is a variation so they do not get discouraged when they show off their new line dance to their friends.

Expand your teaching arena. Teach at mixers and social functions. But be sure to know yourself and your limitations, and take care of yourself. Too much teaching can burn you out if you get stressed.

When teaching private lessons, adjust your instruction to the student's age and ability. Find out as much as you can about the student's likes and dislikes, especially the line dances she or he wants to learn. For example, is this person taking lessons as a crash course before a wedding? Play music your private student likes.

Attitude shows! Don't ever compete or show you are better than your students. Remember, there will always be someone better and worse than you. You are there for them to help them achieve their goals. So enjoy, and your students will too.

Appendix A
Complete List of Line Dances

Listed here are the names of line dances published when I wrote this book. My sources included a poll of dance clubs throughout the United States, country-western magazines, television, dance videos, and correspondence with other dance instructors.

Abilene
Abilene Walk
Achy Breaky
Acorn
(A) Fifth of Beethoven
Air Conditioner Blues
A.K.A. the Plum
Alabama
Alabama Swingin'
Alabama Super Slide
Alberta Rose
Algamotion
All My X's Live in Texas
All Points West
Alley Cat
Alpine
Amarillo
Amos Moses
Angel Fire
Anthracite Rose Stroll
Appaloosa's Christmas Waltz
Applejack
Arkansas Bus Stop
Arkansas Stomp
Arlene
Armadillo
Austin
Back "40"
Back Tracking
Backwalk
Backwards Shuffle
Bad Bad Leroy (Brown)
Bad Bob Strut
Baja Bayou
Baltimore Bustle
Baltimore Bustle, The New

Bangue Boogie
Barkerville Strut
Barkley's Stroll
Bar None Strut
Barnyard Hustle
Bar Room Romeo
Bar Stool Swing
B-Bop
"BC"
Berlin Boogie
BG Boogie Woogie
Big Heart
Big Valley Stomp
Bikini Shuffle
Birmingham Rock
BJ Hustle
Black Jack
Black Velvet
Blazin' Saddle Stomp
Blue Beat
Blue Jeans Polka
Board Walk
Bocephus
Boise Boot Scoot
Bonanza
Boom
Boone Walk
Bootleg Jazz
Boot Scoot Boogie
Boot Scoot Boogie II
Boot Scooters' Kick
Boots "N" Buckles Break
Bop
Boppers Strut
Bossa Nova
Boston Bump

Box Car
Box Waltz
Branding Iron
Brewsters Bump
British Cowgirl Hustle
Bronc Buster
Bronco Stomp
Brown Bear Hustle
Brown Dogger
Brymho Fantasy
"Bubba"
Buckaroo
Buffalo Boogie
Buffalo Rose
Buick
Bulldog Boogie
Bull Whip
Bump and Grind
Bunk House Boogie
Burning
Bus Stop
Butterfly Waltz
Cactus Belle
Cactus Flower
Cadillac Style
Cajun
Cajun Cowgirl Boogie
Cajun Cross
Calendar Girl
Calgary Shuffle
California 10-Step
California Bus Stop
California Coast
California Monorail
California Strut
California Tanglefoot

Candida
Candy Man
Car Wash
Casino/Royal Casino
Century Bay
Cha-Cha
Cha-Cha Fever
Cha-Cha Teaser
Chaps
Charlotte's Cha-Cha
Cheatin' Heart
Cherokee Kick
Chesterfield
Cheyenne
Chicago Bus Stop
Chicago City
Chicken Boogie
Chicken Four Corners
Chinook
Chisholm Stomp
Chocolate City Hustle
Chuck-A-Lou
Chuckwagon Cha-Cha
Chuckwagon Special
Cicero Swamp Stomp
Cimarron
Cimarron Boogie
Cimarron Stomp
Cimarron Stroll
Cincinnati
Circle Up
Cleopatra
Clinton's Little Rock
Clover Hall Stomp
Clyde
Clyde Slyde
Coca-Cola Hornet Buzz
Cold Sweat
Coles Crossing
Colorado Shuffle
Colorado Stomp
Continental
Contradiction
Copperhead Road
Corkscrew
Corral Crossing
Cortland (NY) Grapevine
Cotton Mouth

Country Boy
Country Club
Country DJ
Country Girl
Country Hoedown
Country Lady
Country Selection
Country Stomp
Country Street
Country Strut
Country Line
Country Line Cha-Cha
Country Line Hustle
Courtin'
Cowboy Beat I
Cowboy Boogie
Cowboy Bus Stop
Cowboy Cha-Cha
Cowboy Gallop
Cowboy Hip-Hop
Cowboy Hustle
Cowboy Kick
Cowboy Motion
Cowboy Polka
Cowboy Prance
Cowboy Shuffle
Cowboy Twist
Cowgirl Blues
Cowgirl Cha-Cha
Cowgirl Connection
Cowgirl Hip-Hop
Cowgirl Shuffle
Cowpoke Strut
Cowpony
Cowtown Boogie
Coyote
Coyote Hustle
Crazy 8's
Crazy Horse
Crazy Legs
Crazy T Line Dance
Crooked Stirrup
Cross Fire Shuffle
Crosshitch Cha-Cha
Crossin' Over
Crossover Shuffle
Crusin'
Crusin' Bobtail

Crystal Cowboy
Cucaracha
Cumberland Road Stomp
CW Saloon
CW Waltz
Dallas
Dallas City Stomp
Dallas Hustle
Dallas Shuffle
Dancin' Boots
Dancin' Don's Quick Step
Dancing Cowboy
Dancin' Snowflakes
DC Express
Denver
Desperado
Desperado Slide
Diamond
Ding Dong Daddy
Dirty Hitchhiker
Disco Fever
Disco Walk
Doin' It Country
Do Wah
Dolly
Double Bell Star
Double Cross
Double "D"
Double Dutch Bus
Double Eagle
Double "K"
Double Lonestar
Double R Shuffle
Double Trouble Shuffle
Driftwood
Drop
Dry Gulch Cha-Cha
Duffy Attitude
Duke
Dust Devil
Dust Kicker
Dutchess
Dutchess Hustle
Earthquake
Eight Corners
Eight Corners Eight Count
Eighteen Wheeler
Electric Boogie

Electric Slide
Electric Slide II
El Paso
Elvira
Elvira Cha-Cha
Elvira/Freeze Waltz
Exotic Country
Faith Walk
Fastbreak
Fast Louie
Fatz Careem
Fatz Massé Motion
Fatz Slide Pocket M.D.
Feeling Lucky
Fireman
Fireside Stroll
Five Star Boogie
Flea
Flying Eight
Foot Boogie
Forty-Four Double Cross
Forty-Nine Step
Forty-Two Step
Four Corners
Four Corner Shuffle
Four Star Boogie
Fraser Valley Stomp
Freeze
Freeze II
Funky Cowboy
Fuzzy Duck Slide
Fuzzy Duck Strut
Fuzzy Duck Turn Around
Gabby's Twist
Gardena Gallop
Gator Get Along
G.B. Wiggle
George's Dance
Georgia Bar Dance
Georgia Stomp
Get Rhythm
Ghostbusters
G.I. Jump
Gilley
Ginnie
Givenchy
Gold Coast Special
Golden Waltz

Good Old Days
Grandma's Stroll
Grindstone
Grrr-izzly-R
Gunslinger
Gunslinger Boogie
Gypsy Cowboy
Harlem Shuffle
Hawaiian Hustle
Hayseed Boogie
Heart Breaker Strut
Heartland Express
Heel 'N' Hook
Helen's Left Footen
Henrietta
High Steppin' Country Boogie
Hillbilly Rock
Hi Neighbor!
Hip Hop
Hip-Hop Boogie
Hitch-Hiker
Hitching Post
Hold on Partner
Honey Dipper
Honky Tonk
Honky Tonk Attitude
Honky Tonk Stomp
Honky Tonk Walkin'
Hooked on Country
Hop-Switch Boogie
Horse Feathers
Horseshoe Shuffle
Horsin' Around
Hot Country
Hot Sweat
Hot Sweat Slide
Hot Sweat Turn About
Hully Gully
Hurricane
Hurry Hustle
Illusions Five
In-Cahoot Scoot
In Mexico
Insomnia
Jackie Gleason
Jack Rabbit
Jackson Stomp
Jamaica Farewell

Jeannie K
Jersey Lil
Jersey Lil Boogie
Jive Talkin'
Johnston Country Shuffle
Joker's Wild
Jonny O
J.R. Hustle
Juddin' Line Dance
July Schottische
Just for Kicks
Just Heat
Kansas City
Kansas City Stomp
Kansas Four Corner
Kansas Twister
K-D Shuffle
Kent Square Bus Stop
Kentucky Lariat
Kick 'Em Up
Kickers
Kickers Hustle
Kickin' Corners
Kickin' the Blues
Kickin' Trouble
Kicking the Dust
King Tut Strut
Knightsbridge Strut
Kokomo
K T Hustle
K-Town Boogie
L.A. "Pop" Lock
Laredo Sidewinder
Lariat
L.A. Six Corners
Las Vegas Gambler
L.A. Walk
Lawndale Loco-Motion
Lazy Eight Waltz
Lazy J. Special
L.B. Lariat
Leapin' Lizard
LeDoux Shuffle
Little Black Book
Little Blue Shoe
Little Circle
Little Latin
Little Sister

Lobo
Lone Star
Lookin' Like Country
Louie
Louisiana Louis
Louisiana Saturday Night
Louisiana Slap
Lucas McCain
Lusty Lady
Lynda
Manitoba Hustle
Massachusetts South 40
Matador
M.C. Bump
McKenzie Stomp
Mercury Red Devil
Mexican Corn
Minnesota Boogie
Missouri Flip
Monorail
Montana
Montana Four Corner
Montana Hustle
Montana Stomp
Montclair Stomp
Moonshine Shuffle
Moonwalk
Mule
Mustang
Mustang Salley
Nagella Slide
Nanaimo Stomp
Nashville Clod
Neon Cha-Cha
Neon Cowboy
Nevada
New Balling the Jack
New Jersey Flying Eight
New Orleans Rock
New York, New York
New York Schottische
Night Chicago Died
Night Run
No Name
Northbound
Northern Lights
Northside Cha-Cha
NTA Express

Oakie Turnaround
Oakridge
OK Corral
Oklahoma Stomp (Okie Stomp)
Oklahoma Twist
Old Glory
Old Man/Shuffle/Bus Stop
One Step Forward
Oregon Express
Osan
Our Dennis
Outlaw
Outlaw Polka
Paddle Wheel
Palace Slap
Pasadena
Pata Pata
Pender Step
Pennine Way
Penny Rock
Phoenix Circle
Pigeon Toe Four Corners
Ponderosa
Ponderosa Strut
Pony Express
Pookie
Poor White Boy
Popcorn
Power Jam
Prairie Dog
Prairie Schottische
Prairie Twist
Prancing Pony
Queen City
Queen of Memphis
Queen's Waltz
Ramble
Ramblin'
Randall's Rag
Rawhide
Red Bandana
Red Hot
Redneck Boogie
Redneck Girl
Redondo Beach Roundup
Redwood City Hustle
Reggae
Reggae Boogie

Reggae Cowboy
Reggae Cowboy II
Reno Roundup
Restless Feet
Revenuer
Rhinestone Cowboy
Rhinestone Cowboy Stomp
"Ricky"
Ricochet
R.J.
Rock
Rockabilly
Rockabilly Boogie
Rocking Horse
Rockin' in the Smokies
Rockin' Magnolia Stomp
Rocky Hustle
Rodeo
Rodeo Connection
Rodeo Strut
Roll Back the Rug
Rolling R
Romeo
Romeo Stroll
R.O. Twist
Rough-Rider
Roulette Wheel
Round About Country
Round Up
Ruby Baby
Ruthie
Saddle Stomp
Sagebrush
Saloon Strut
Salty Dog Rag
Sam's Town Hustle
San Diego Shuffle
San Francisco Hustle
San Jose Sashay
Saturday Night Fever Hustle
Schottische
Scootin' Boot Boogie
Scuffletown Shuffle
Scuffletown Suzie Q
Seattle Eight
Seminole Wind
Serpentine Waltz
Shadow

Shag Shuffle
Sheffield Shuffle
Shiloh Turn-Around
Shoo Bert Shuffle
Shorthorn Boogie
Shorts
Shotgun
Showdown
Shuffle
Shundo Shuffle
Side by Side
Side Hitch
Side Kick
Sidesaddle
Sidestep
Sidewinder
Silverado
Silver Buckle
Silverdale Shuffle
Silver Dollar
Silver Dollar Slide
Silvermoon Boogie
Silver Stomper
Simple Country
Simple Man
Single's Two Step
Six Corners
Six Step (Line Dance)
Sixteen Step Line
Skat
Ski Bumpus
S Kickin'
Skip
Slam Dunk
Slap Happy
Slap Leather
Slapping Chocolate
Slappin' Leather
Sleazy Slide
Slip Knot
Slippin' Around
Slo Cadillac
Slush/Slosh/Keep Moving
Smokin' Boots
Smooth
Snakebite
Snoopy
Snowbird Shuffle

Sod Buster
Solitary Waltz
Soul City Variation
South 40
Southeast Hustle
Southern Moon
Southside Shuffle
Southside Waltz
Spam
Spanish Two Step
Split Rail
Spur's Stomp
Squash
Stagecoach Hustle
Stardust
Startin' Over Blues
Staying Alive
Step "N" Time Strut
St. Louis Shag
Stormy Stagger
Stray Cat
Stray Cat Strut
Stretchin' Denim
Strokin' T.C.
Strut N' Stroll
Sugar Foot
Sugar Foot Boogie
Sugar Foot Shuffle
Sundance
Sunday Stroll
Super Freak
Sutter Street Strut
Swamp Rat
Sweet Gypsy Rose
Sweetheart Hustle
Sweet Shelley Shuffle
Sweetwater
Swinger
Swingin'
Swingin' Coyote
Swingin' Doors
Swing-N
Tahoe Stomp
Tahoe Twist
Take a Little Trip
Tamborelli
Tangle Foot
TCR Shuffle

T.C. Slide
Tennessee Birdwalk
Tennessee Stroll
Tennessee Tornado
Tennessee Twister
Tennessee Wig Walk
Ten Pretty Girls
Tequila
Terry's Shuffle
Texas Backslide
Texas Cha-Cha
Texas Four Corners
Texas Freeze
Texas Ranger
Texas Shuffle
Texas Stomp
Texas Tap
Texas Tease
Texas Twist
Thunderbolt
Thunderfoot
Tie a Yellow Ribbon
Tiny Bubbles
T.K. Turnaround
TLC Boogie
Tomato Patch Shuffle
Top Rail Boogie
Tornado
Torrance Trot
Torrance Twist
Trashy Women
Traveler
Traveler Three
Traveling Four Corners
Triple "T"
Triples
Tropicana Parking Lot
Trouble
T's Shuffle
"T" Step
Tulsa Time
Tulsa Tumbleweed
Tulsa Twist
Tulsa Twister
Tumbleweed
Turnin' 30
Tush Push
Tutu

Twelfth Street Rag
Twister
Two Corner
Uh Huh Connection
Ukiah 20 Step Toot Toot
Valley Rock
Vancouver Boogie
Victor
Video Blues
Virgo Strut
Walk
Walkin'
Walkin' in the Line
Walkin' Outside the Line
Walkin' Wazi
Waltz Across Texas
Waltz Line Dance
Wanderer
Watergate
Wellston Crossing Boogie

West "40" Break
Western Boogie
Western Electric
Western Express
Western Girls
Western Sizzler
Western Tango
Wheels
Whiskey Blues
Whiskey River
White Toro
Whitewater Hustle
Wild Bump
Wild Card
Wild Country Buckshot
Wildman
Wild West
Wild Wild West Boogie
Wild Willie
Willamette Hustle

Willie Walk
Willies
Winchester
Winchester Cathedral/Skate
Windsor Waltz
Winter Wonderland
Wooden Nickel
Wrangler
Wrangler Jeans
Wrangler Waltz
XLT Ranger
Ya Ya
Ying Yang
Yochim
Ziggie
Zydeco Lady

Appendix B
Suggested Music

Here is a list of line dances with selected popular music, compiled in our national survey.

Dance Name	Song Title	Artist
Achy Breaky	"Achy Breaky Heart"	Billy Ray Cyrus
Alley Cat	"Dumas Walker"	The Kentucky Headhunters
Amos Moses	"Amos Moses"	Jerry Reed
Barn Dance	"Wild Wild West"	The Escape Club
Bird Dance	"Bird Dance"	The Emeralds
Black Velvet	"Two of a Kind"	Garth Brooks
Boot Scoot Boogie	"Kiss Me in the Car"	John Berry
Boot Scoot Boogie II	"Boot Scootin' Boogie"	Brooks & Dunn
Breezy	"Easy Come, Easy Go"	George Strait
Bunny Hop	"The Bunny Hop"	Ray Anthony
Bus Stop	"Stayin' Alive"	Bee Gees
Clyde	"Fast As You"	Dwight Yoakum
Conga	"Hot, Hot, Hot"	Buster Poindexter
Cotton Eyed Joe	"Cotton Eyed Joe"	Midnight Rodeo
Country Strut	"God Bless Texas (mix)"	Little Texas
Cowboy Boogie	"Have Mercy"	The Judds
Cowboy Cha-Cha	"Gulf of Mexico"	Clint Black
Cowboy Hip-Hop	"Elevate My Mind"	Stereo MC's
Cowboy Hustle	"Wrong Side of Memphis"	Trisha Yearwood
Cowboy Motion	"Chattahoochee"	Alan Jackson
Crazy 8's	"Friends in Low Places"	Garth Brooks
Dallas Shuffle	"Why Not Me"	The Judds
Double Dutch Bus	"Drive South"	Suzy Bogguss
Eight Corners	"Watch Me"	Lorrie Morgan
Electric Slide	"Electric Slide"	Melinda Johnson

Dance Name	Song Title	Artist
Electric Slide II	"Electric Slide"	Grandmaster Slice
Elvira	"Elvira"	Oak Ridge Boys
Flying Eight	"Prop Me up Beside the Jukebox"	Joe Diffie
Freeze	"I Feel Lucky"	Mary Chapin Carpenter
Freeze II	"Mountain Music"	Alabama
Funky Cowboy	"Funky Cowboy"	Ronnie McDowell
Ghostbusters	"Ghostbusters"	Ghostbusters Soundtrack
Hip Hop	"Free Your Mind"	En Vogue
Hitch-Hiker	"Bop"	Dan Seals
Hokey Pokey	"Hokey Pokey"	Mike Stanglin
Honky Tonk Stomp	"Honky Tonk Attitude"	Joe Diffie
Hooked on Country	"Ain't Nothin' Wrong With the Radio"	Aaron Tippin
Horseshoe Shuffle	"Heartland"	George Strait
Kokomo	"Kokomo"	Beach Boys
LeDoux Shuffle	"Cadillac Ranch"	Chris LeDoux
Longhorn Special	"I Feel Lucky"	Mary Chapin Carpenter
Louie	"Redneck Girl"	Bellamy Brothers
Reggae Cowboy	"Get Into Reggae Cowboy"	Bellamy Brothers
Reggae Cowboy II	"Let Your Love Flow"	Bellamy Brothers
Rockabilly Boogie	"Some Kind of Trouble"	Tanya Tucker
Romeo	"Romeo"	Dolly Parton
Slappin' Leather	"Reckless"	Alabama
Sleazy Slide	"American Made"	Oak Ridge Boys
Stray Cat Strut	"Walk Softly on This Heart"	The Kentucky Headhunters
Stroll	"The Stroll"	Diamonds
Ten-Step	"Liza Jane"	Vince Gill
Tennessee Stroll	"Take It Back"	Reba McEntire
Thunderfoot	"Brand New Man"	Brooks & Dunn
Traveling Cha-Cha	"Love Is Still Alive"	Midnight Rodeo
Traveling Four Corners	"Money in the Bank"	John Anderson
Tumbleweed	"Rockin' With the Rhythm"	The Judds
Tush Push	"Two of a Kind"	Garth Brooks
Walkin' Wazi	"Thank God for You"	Sawyer Brown

Resources

For videos of line dances in this book and information about Christy Lane's workshops and performances:

    Let's Do It! Productions
    P.O. Box 5483
    Spokane, WA 99205
    509-235-6555

For information on portable cassette players and compact disc players:

    Sportime
    Select Service and Supply Co., Inc.
    One Sportime Way
    Atlanta, GA 30340
    800-283-5700

For information on professional sound systems:

    Steve Springer
    Hoffman's Music
    P.O. Box 385
    Spokane, WA 99210
    509-328-3888

For information regarding line dance instruction certification:

    Gwen Hyatt
    Desert Southwest Fitness
    3220 E. Via Celeste
    Tucson, AZ 85718
    800-873-6759

For information regarding music licensing:

    American Society of Composers, Authors and Publishers
    One Lincoln Plaza
    New York, NY 10023
    212-595-3050

    Broadcast Music, Inc.
    320 W. 57th St.
    New York, NY 10019
    212-586-2000

For a listing of country-western dance clubs:

    The Official Country Music Directory
    Entertainment Media Corporation
    P.O. Box 2772
    Palm Springs, CA 92262
    619-322-3858

For information regarding line dance competitions:

> *Country Dance Lines* Magazine
> Drawer 139
> Woodacre, CA 94973
> 415-488-0154

For the latest music list:

> See *Billboard* magazine's ratings at your local music store

For aerobic music:

> Dynamix Music Service
> 733 W. 40th St., Ste. 10
> Baltimore, MD 21211
> 800-843-6499

> Power Productions
> 1303 S. Swaner Rd.
> Salt Lake City, UT 84104
> 800-777-BEAT

For information about aerobic certification and liability insurance:

> American Council on Exercise
> 5820 Oberlin Dr., Ste. 102
> San Diego, CA 92121
> 619-535-8227

> Aerobics and Fitness Association of America
> 15250 Ventura Blvd., Ste. 200
> Sherman Oaks, CA 91403
> 800-446-AFAA

More great dance resources

Social Dance

Steps to Success

Judy Patterson Wright, PhD

1992 • Paper • 176 pp • Item PWRI0449
ISBN 0-88011-449-5 • $15.95 ($22.95 Canadian)

Social Dance Music Cassettes

Original Music by Richard Gardzina

Social Dance: Steps to Success gives beginning dancers simple, step-by-step instructions for learning five popular social dance styles: Swing, Cha-Cha, Polka, Waltz, Fox Trot.

What makes this book unique is the step-by-step progression that teaches simple skills, then builds on those skills to develop creative dance routines. As you progress, you'll learn how to execute basic steps, communicate with your partner, lead and follow, move from one dance position to another, and create your own dance sequences.

Social Dance: Steps to Success will help you get started, make steady progress, practice in performance contexts, and adjust to various dance situations.

Special soundsheet included

A special feature of *Social Dance: Steps to Success* is the soundsheet, bound right into the book. Play it on a turntable, and you have 18 minutes of music that complements the lessons and drills in the book.

Companion music cassettes

Five cassette tapes are also available—one for each dance style—that provide 30 more minutes of music to practice with.

Social Dance Music Set (5-cassette package)
Item MGAR0191 • $39.95 ($59.95 Canadian)

Swing Music Cassette
Item MGAR0192 • $8.95 ($13.50 Canadian)

Waltz Music Cassette
Item MGAR0193 • $8.95 ($13.50 Canadian)

Cha-Cha Music Cassette
Item MGAR0194 • $8.95 ($13.50 Canadian)

Fox-Trot Music Cassette
Item MGAR0195 • $8.95 ($13.50 Canadian)

Polka Music Cassette
Item MGAR0196 • $8.95 ($13.50 Canadian)

Prices are subject to change.

**Human
Kinetics**

2335

To order the above book and cassettes, use the appropriate telephone number/address shown on page ii of this book, or **call toll-free in the U.S. (1-800-747-4457)**

Line dancing videos by Christy Lane

These dynamic line dance videos bring *Christy Lane's Complete Book of Line Dancing* to life!

- •*Line Dancing*—Volume I
    Includes Freeze, Electric Slide, Slappin' Leather, Tush Push, Alley Cat, and Boot Scoot.
- •*Line Dancing*—Volume II
    Features even more great dances: Achy Breaky, Cowboy Boogie, Cowboy Cha Cha, Elvira, and Walkin' Wazie.

- •*Hot New Line Dances*
    Learn the Cowboy Hip-Hop, Black Velvet, Tumbleweed, and the popular Hip Hop.
- •*More Hot New Line Dances*
    The Cowboy Motion, Romeo, Ghostbusters, and the new Boot Scootin' Boogie II are included.

To order any of Christy Lane's videos, write to Let's Do It Productions, P.O. Box 5483, Spokane, WA 99205, or call 509-235-6555.